Felucca *sailing on the Nile, Luxor, Egypt.*

(Cover) Mondari woman with forehead tribal identification scar lines and decorative small dots, south of Tali Post, Sudan.

(Pages 2-3) Great Pyramids of Giza, seen from Cairo, Egypt.

(Pages 4-5) El Molo children beside village huts, east shore of Lake Turkana, Kenya.

For Anthony & Mary Bowen Caputo

"You're the Nile,
You're the Tower of Pisa,
You're the smile
On the Mona Lisa."
—Cole Porter, "You're the Top"

For giving me the opportunities to look and for helping me to see, for guidance through these and other travels, for enduring friendship, and for spiritual, emotional, and at times even physical sustenance, I am especially thankful to: Margaret MacLean, Bob Gilka, Barbie Allen, Bill Garrett, Lilian Davidson, Don Gummer & Meryl Streep, Nick & Martie Proffitt, Dave & Barbara Wood, David Lamb & Sandy Northrop, Hugo van Lawick, Mel Scott, Declan Haun, Ann Turner, Mimi Conway & Dennis Houlihan.

Published by Thomasson-Grant, Inc.,
Frank L. Thomasson III and John F. Grant, Directors;
Megan R. Youngquist, Art Director.
Designed by Jim Gibson
Edited by Carolyn M. Clark

Library of Congress Catalog Number: 87-40672
ISBN 0-934738-36-X
Color separations by Pioneer Graphic through CGI (Malaysia) Sdn. Bhd.
Printed in the United States by Hoechstetter Printing, Inc.
Any inquiries should be directed to Thomasson-Grant, Inc.,
One Morton Drive, Suite 500, Charlottesville, Virginia 22901,
telephone (804) 977-1780.

Library of Congress Cataloging-in-Publication Data

Caputo, Robert
    Journey up the Nile.

    1. Nile River Valley—Description and travel.
2. Caputo, Robert—Journeys—Nile River Valley.
I. Title.
DT115.C28 1988   916.2'0455   87-40672
ISBN 0-934738-36-X

THOMASSON-GRANT

JOURNEY UP
THE NILE

ROBERT CAPUTO

INTRODUCTION

I first went to Africa 17 years ago as a traveler with no particular expectations and scant knowledge beyond that gleaned from history and geography lessons in school. My image of Africa was vague, a mysterious place inhabited by fantastical beasts and strange people, an exotic backdrop for comic book and movie adventures. In my initial wanderings, I found the continent appealing, largely because it is exotic, so different from the world I grew up in that I was forced to re-evaluate the way I looked at everything, including myself.

I have spent most of my time there ever since. For several years I lived in Kenya, making pictures of the wildlife that abounds in East Africa, and later working as a freelance photographer for *Time, Life,* and other magazines. The assignments for *Time* especially enabled me to travel throughout the continent and learn something of the political, economic, and social problems with which Africa's new nations contend. For the past eight years, I have been writing and photographing stories for *National Geographic,* which has provided me the time and resources to explore more of Africa than is reflected in the all-too-frequently depressing news.

This book is mainly an account of experiences from one of several trips I made while working on *National Geographic* stories, an eight-month journey during which

Rendille warriors and Caputo, Kenya.

I drove along the Nile from its mouth in the Mediterranean Sea to its source deep in the heart of Africa. The people I met offered me glimpses into their lives and into something more enduring than the political structures recently erected around them. The storybook image of my youth has been reshaped by the realities of modern Africa, but has not lost its allure. Quite the contrary; though much of Africa is harsh or mundane, even more of it is compelling and mysterious in ways I could not have imagined.

It seems inconceivable now, in an age when spaceborne cameras peer into every corner of the planet, that only 130 years ago the Nile posed the most elusive geographical puzzle on earth. The ancient Egyptians were utterly dependent on the Nile's annual flood for thousands of years; if the Nile failed, Egypt starved. But they had no idea whence it came, and could not control or even predict their very lifeblood. The insecurity this engendered must have played a large part in the evolution of their religious and governmental institutions. The Egyptians, and later the Roman Emperor Nero, sent expeditions upstream to find the source of the Nile, but they either perished in that unknown land or returned defeated by its deserts and swamps.

By the middle of the 19th century, European geographers had mapped much of the world. The coast of Africa was charted, but the interior remained a vast void, a terra incognita filled on the maps with drawings of fanciful people and beasts.

This mystery did not sit well with the Victorians who believed that nothing in nature could withstand the taming and civilizing hand of man—particularly Victorian man, the very "crown of creation." That such a large portion of the globe remained un- known was intolerable to these gentlemen, and they were certain that by applying themselves and their newfound "scientific method" to the task, the puzzle would be solved. It was the last flourish of the age of exploration, and the names of the players—Livingstone, Stanley, Burton, Speke, and Baker—are the stuff of legends.

I am not an anthropologist, geographer, or academic of any sort. I researched the places I traveled as well as I could, but do not pretend that my experiences or the people I encountered are necessarily representative. Chance plays the leading role in travel, with the traveler's moods and attitudes not far behind. Another

Caputo camped for the night, Sudan.

person on exactly the same route would no doubt write a completely different account. With just a slight change of timing, my own experiences could have been quite different; a walk down a street might result in a mugging or, if taken a few minutes later, an enduring friendship. Chance is the great allure of travel; remaining open to it is the great challenge.

I drove up the Nile in a Mercedes four-wheel drive vehicle that I collected at the factory in Germany, where it was fitted out to carry everything I might need during the eight months it was my home. I spent a week in Stuttgart being briefed on routine maintenance and buying supplies.

After I became comfortable with the vehicle, I set off one morning, in the winter of 1983, across the Alps. Other drivers on the autobahn honked and stared, gesturing as if to question where I might be going in such a rig. It made me wonder just what I had gotten myself into. I was about to drive, all by myself, through lands where I did not know the languages, where roads, fuel, and mechanics were often nonexistent, and where civil wars raged with death tolls in the hundreds of thousands. All the beasts in that terra incognita loomed ahead of me. I searched for a reasonable excuse to turn around, but found none. The only thing to do was continue on to Venice where I would meet the ship that would carry me across the Mediterranean Sea to the mouth of the Nile.

Salisbury, Connecticut

EGYPT

*I*t is difficult to approach Egypt without being overwhelmed by the past. The images of its history—the Sphinx, the Great Pyramids, Tutankhamun—are so familiar and powerful that they dominate the mind much as they dominate the Egyptian countryside. The monuments of antiquity lure thousands of foreigners each year. Tourists come to see the Egypt that used to be.

While not ignoring the antiquities, which is impossible in any case, I wanted to see more. But Egypt is set up for tourists, and most Egyptians expect foreigners to act like them, herded from temple to tomb to hotel, Evian water tucked under an arm. Tourists glimpse Egypt through the window of a bus or from the deck of a luxury cruise ship plying the Nile. Sometimes it seems quaint—robed figures lifting water from the Nile with primitive, weight-pivoted *shadufs*. Usually, though, the tourist finds Egypt dirty, noisy, crowded, and bothersome.

It is hard for any place to live up to expectations founded on former glory, especially glory as former as Egypt's. I overheard many tourists ask the question: "How could these people have built such amazing things thousands of years ago? Look at the country now." It seems like a fall from grace, an unwelcome reminder of the mortality of our own constructs. (One popular tourist attraction is the toppled statue of Ramses II, known to the Greeks as Ozymandias, which inspired Shelley's poem about vainglory.) I am afraid I compared present and ancient Egypt, too, but tried to remind myself that doing so was both irrelevant and mean.

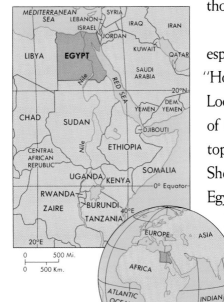

Egypt was in many ways the most difficult part of my trip. Not physically—tourism makes it an easy place to be, with plenty of hotels, services, and roads. That was just the problem: I too easily fell prey to the comforts and amenities, and had difficulty tearing myself away from them to spend time with the farmers and fishermen who live along the Nile. The river's particular ecology gave birth to Egypt in the first place; it is the reason the monuments exist, and it sustains the state today.

I started my travels in the Delta, the huge triangle of land between Cairo and the Mediterranean Sea that the ancients called "the bud of the lotus." The long, thin Nile Valley to the south is the stem. The Delta and the Valley account for only 3 percent of Egypt's land, but are home to 96 percent of her 48 million people. It is crowded.

I spent the first few days driving around, trying to get a feel for the place and

(Facing) Fisherman carrying his catch, Lake Idku.

overcome both the culture shock and shyness that hamper me at the beginning of a trip of this sort. I had no problem making contact with people. The Delta is so crowded that it was impossible to find an isolated camping spot. I slept in towns next to police stations or at the edge of villages. Few foreigners visit the Delta, so my vehicle and I were unusual sights; whenever I stopped at a farm or a village, people immediately dropped whatever they were doing and either stood staring or rushed over to have a closer look. All this attention made taking candid photographs rather difficult, but eased the transition, and helped me

Sphinx, Giza.

overcome my own hesitations.

"Egypt," as the Greek historian Hecataeus observed in 450 B.C., "is the gift of the Nile." Except for the Delta and the Valley, Egypt is desert. They are habitable only because the Nile, over the ages, has brought millions of tons of silt down from central Africa, depositing it in thin strips along its banks during the floods, and spreading it out to create new land where it meets the sea. The Delta is simply 8,500 square miles of mud.

Every inch of the perfectly flat land seemed to be cultivated, except the islands of houses where the *fellahin* (farmers) live, clustered together to take up as little room as possible. I frequently got lost trying to navigate the narrow roads that wind through the maze of fields and irrigation canals, and stopped often to ask directions in broken Arabic.

Donkeys, oxen, and water buffalos strained under their loads, or tramped in ceaseless circles around the pivots of creaky water wheels. People crowded the roads, gathered at markets, stooped in the fields. With muddy hands they opened and closed the small earthen dams that channel water through the intricate irrigation ditches. In the canals people bathed, and women hiked up their long, full skirts, squatting to wash dishes and clothes. Young girls fetched drinking water.

This timeless picture had been my preconception—thousands of years ago the scene must have been much the same. But the reality is less romantic. People dump refuse and relieve themselves in the canals. Since the Aswan High Dam stopped the annual Nile flood, the canals have become clogged with grass and reeds. Bilharzia, a liver fluke that can be fatal, abounds in the still water where its intermediate host, a snail, thrives. The fluke enters humans through the skin, and the eggs are passed by people back into the canals. It seems an easy enough cycle to break, but habit and the lack of any other facilities keep it alive.

I spent one afternoon sitting on the stoop of a small shop with some farmers, taking turns drawing on a tall water pipe charged with tobacco and hashish. Over many cups of very sweet tea, and with sign language, I pieced together a bit of what they were telling me: "The earth is good, there is plenty of water, the sun is warm. Allah has blessed us here in the Delta. We have food to eat and some to sell. What more could a man want in this world?"

CAIRO SPRAWLS across the Nile at the junction of the Delta and the Valley, trying desperately to accommodate its ten million people. It seemed to me as I drove in that they were all in their cars, eagerly burning up the ten-cent-a-gallon gas. Rush hour in Cairo is all hours; the city appears perpetually on the verge of gridlock. Throngs of people, in both Arab and western dress, pack the sidewalks. Buses are stuffed to overflowing with passengers hanging half out the windows. Traffic lights are ignored. Drivers seem to believe that vehicles will not function properly unless the horns are engaged, and lights have but two positions, off and blinding.

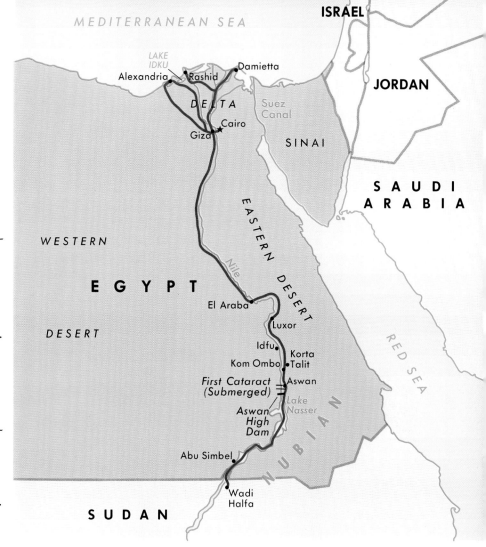

My routine in Cairo was to spend the middle of the day pursuing the elusive bureaucrats from whom I sought interviews and permits for travel and photography. In the early mornings and late afternoons, when the light is good, I made photographs of the city and nearby sites.

One evening I climbed up to the Citadel, a fortress built in the 12th century. Cairo stretched across the Nile to the Great Pyramids at Giza, thrown into relief by the setting sun. Hundreds of mosques, some nearly as old as Islam itself, thrust their ornate minarets into the orange sky above rooftops where laundry fluttered and women cooked over open fires. Calls to prayer echoed down narrow alleys crammed with people, cars, donkey carts, and street vendors selling everything from rabbits and goats to boom boxes. The air was full of exhaust, smoke, dust, and noises: traffic roaring, voices haggling over prices, chickens squawking, donkeys being beaten.

And everywhere people. Cairo's population is growing by a million people a year, and already they occupy rooftops, hallways, sidewalks, and dinghies moored to the banks of the Nile. They live in the city's garbage dump and in and around the tombs of graveyards. Trash is everywhere; sheltered walls become repositories for human waste. Cairo's water, sewage, electrical, and telephone systems, built to service the 1929 population of 200,000, are strained.

The poverty is hard for a visitor to take, but I could easily seek refuge in the hotel. Cairenes have no escape. Some have learned to make their livings by accosting tourists, and it is impossible for a foreigner in Cairo not to be pestered with various ingenious scams. The constant badgering made me suspicious of everyone, and I probably acted churlishly toward people who may have been sincere, insulting them and robbing myself of the kind of experience for which, after all, I was there.

Modern graveyard and Great Pyramids, Giza.

Most Cairenes, though, have little contact with foreigners, and, despite the conditions in the city, have somehow held onto the kindness and equanimity I had found among the farmers of the Delta. They put up with the intrusiveness of my camera and my questions without complaint.

TRAVELING UP the Nile Valley from Cairo to Aswan is like driving through a thin farm along an exceedingly long irrigation ditch. Blue, green, brown—at the center, the Nile; along it fields sometimes not more than a few yards wide; then, as far as the eye can see east and west, the barren deserts. The road winds through the fields, or draws a black line between them and the sands, passing villages built beyond the reach of the flood in the days before the Aswan High Dam.

For thousands of years, the farmers in the Nile Valley practiced basin agriculture, relying on the annual flood to water and fertilize their fields. Each year, rains in the African interior caused August floods that covered the fields, where earthen dams retained the water for 40 to 60 days. The farmers then broke the dams and planted their crops in the rich, wet silt left behind. Harvest in May was followed by the hot summer, when the river again began to rise.

But the floods could be menacing. Too low a flood reduced the cultivated area by half, bringing famine; too high a flood swept through the valley, wiping out villages, destroying fields, and bringing epidemics and plagues.

By the early 19th century, living with this uncertainty had become intolerable. The rapidly expanding population required more food, and the Khedive's treasury needed money from cash crops like cotton and sugar cane. Barrages and canals were built; water management was refined. But in the period after World War II, Egypt's capacity to produce food by basin agriculture peaked. Not another kernel of wheat or boll of cotton could be squeezed from the land. The nation needed a radical new concept.

Colonel Gamal Abdel Nasser decided against a scheme to control the Nile at its sources (Lake Tana in Ethiopia for the Blue Nile, Lakes Victoria and Albert in Uganda for the White) as too politically uncertain. Such a plan would have put Egypt at the mercy of upstream states, which might threaten to withhold precious water, or release it suddenly, devastating the Nile Valley. Nasser wanted control of the river to lie completely within Egypt's borders.

The United States and other western countries balked at the idea of constructing the High Dam until studies could determine its potential effects. Nasser did not want to wait, and in 1960 the Soviet Union began work. The dam now captures high floods, and droughts, such as the one which caused famine in Ethiopia in 1983-84, no longer threaten Egypt. Lake Nasser, the great reservoir behind the dam, stores two years of water that is released slowly, evenly, throughout the year. Perennial agriculture has replaced basin. The Nile is an irrigation ditch.

I stopped at a lot of farms in the Valley. As in the Delta, my presence was disruptive. Adults set aside their work, kids constantly tried to get into the picture. When I was too close to the tourist sites, they screamed, "Bakshish" (gift), before I even said hello. But by staying long enough for the novelty to wear off, and drinking the tea I was invariably offered, I was able to get some idea of how people lived, and ask about the effects of the High Dam. Everywhere I heard how much better things were: three crops a year instead of one, money from cash crops like sugar cane, electricity for domestic comfort and more efficient irrigation, and no uncertainty.

Saqia (waterwheel) turned by an ox to irrigate village fields, El Awamia, south of Luxor.

"We are safe now," Amin Ibrahim told me at his farm near Luxor. "Before the dam we were obsessed with the flood. Would it be too high or too low? I used to plant my crop and never know if I would harvest. Now there is no fear; we know there will be water, and just how much there will be."

But no flood means no silt, so farmers must buy chemical fertilizers which add salt to the river, already more saline because of enormous evaporation from Lake Nasser. Vegetation clogs canals and riverbanks because the river has no force. Clear water gouges the riverbed in a way silt-rich water did not. The subsurface water table no longer fluctuates, but is high and constant, so the fields do not drain into the river but rather lose water through evaporation, leaving salt on the surface. Amin pointed out spots where salt glistened on the soil, where crops will not grow.

"There are some prices to pay since the dam was built," he remarked. "But our lives are better than before, and that is the important thing. It is what we call progress."

The High Dam will, for a while, enable food production to keep up with Egypt's 2.7 percent annual population growth. Farmers raise cash crops, and previously nonarable land can be cultivated. But it seems to me that there is more to it than salinity, coastal erosion, water tables, irrigation, and food production. The Nile fertilized Egypt for millennia—and not just the fields. Developing technologies to utilize and cooperating to share one resource, the Nile flood, led to the centralization of government and the birth of Egyptian civilization. The grandeur that Egyptians point to with pride, and that so enthralls the rest of us, was born of man's relationship, physical and spiritual, with the unknowable river. The Nile was arbiter of life and death in Egypt. Now there is no mystery, neither adulation nor fear. Man controls the river.

These were ramblings in my journal, a tangent I went off on, as often happened, while eating dinner alone in a hotel. When I asked Amin Ibrahim, as I had asked every farmer and fisherman I spent time with in the Valley, what the Nile meant to him, if he had any stories about the river, he looked at me as if I were crazy. "It is just there," he said. "It brings water to our fields."

AT LUXOR, known in ancient times as Thebes, I gave myself over to being a tourist. Cruise ships lined the waterfront, tour buses and gaudy horse carts crowded the broad avenue along the river. The town's market was jammed not with farmers buying necessities, but with tourists seeking souvenirs. For me it was a time of taking organized tours, buying entrance tickets to the sites, standing in lines, tipping guides, fending off hawkers and beggars, and occasionally finding a quiet moment to contemplate the splendid monuments that have engendered all the fuss.

Colossi of Memnon, the remains of the mortuary temple of Amenhotep III, west bank of Luxor.

Just north of the town lies Karnak, the great temple complex that covers 62 acres. Known as Ipet-esut, "the most esteemed of places," it was 2,000 years in the making. I spent several days wandering through a maze of obelisks, statues, and gloriously decorated columns and walls. A good part of the time I warded off temple guards who wanted tips for pointing out something obvious, or for taking me somewhere it was their job to keep people from going. Next to the sacred lake I had a soda at a kiosk which the owner proclaimed the "Coca Cola Temple." A cowboy movie on TV and a blaring tape of Dire Straits at one end of an avenue of sphinxes competed for my attention with the gigantic pylon at the other.

In ancient times, most people lived on the east bank of the Nile. Government business was conducted there, and priests looked after the temples built beside the river. The west bank, where the sun set, was the place of mortuary temples and tombs, the land of the dead. I slept there in my roof tent at the edge of the desert, feeling as if I had the whole place to myself—the tourists did not arrive from their hotels across the river until about 9:30 in the morning.

Awakening early, I climbed a path to the top of the rocky cliffs above Hatshepsut's temple, watching the sun rise over the eastern desert, its red glow reflected in the thin ribbon of the Nile. The fields and desert were shrouded in mist. I could just make out the Colossi of Memnon and the walls and pillars of the Ramesseum on the plain below. Behind me, sunk in the dry hills, lay the Valley of the Kings, where the pharaohs sought refuge for their voyage through eternity.

Even the ancient monuments are being adversely affected by the High Dam. Evaporation from Lake Nasser has brought humidity to the desert air of Upper Egypt for the first time, with as yet unknown consequences for the monuments and their delicate paint. One problem is already visible; because the water table is high, salt-bearing water migrates to the monuments' surfaces. When the water evaporates, the salts crystalize, cracking the stone and often causing it to chip.

Some monuments have been affected much more directly; they are gone. Except for a few that were disassembled and moved at enormous cost, the monuments south of Aswan now lie beneath the waters of Lake Nasser, slowly being buried by the silt that will completely fill the lake in about 500 years.

People lived in the Nile Valley south of Aswan, too; their villages and fields suffered the same fate as the monuments. Sixty thousand Egyptian Nubians were relocated. The government could not move them to similar land north of Aswan, because it had long been occupied. Instead, new villages were built for them in the desert east of the Nile at Kom Ombo.

Woman selling sweet cakes, old Cairo.

NUBIANS ARE a non-Arab people who have inhabited the Nile Valley south of Aswan for thousands of years. In ancient times, they lived beyond Egypt proper; the first cataract at Aswan made the Nile unnavigable and provided the Nubians with a natural barrier to firm rule from the north. But Nubia was always important to Egypt as an avenue for Africa's riches: ivory, incense, slaves, and gold (Nubia comes from the ancient word for gold, *nub*). It was a border region—now rebellious, now subdued.

Modern Nubians look just like their Arab neighbors, speak Arabic, and adhere to Islam. But among themselves they speak Nubian and are very conscious of maintaining a separate identity, though this is increasingly difficult since the loss of their ancestral homeland. Many feel that it is largely due to their "otherness" that the government seemed to have little compunction about sacrificing them to the High Dam.

Nubia was famous for its airy, decoratively painted dwellings made from palm fronds and Nile mud. The new villages are rows of wall-to-wall, cinder-block houses. Although the people have worked to make the houses comfortable and attractive, they do not like living so close to each other and complain that the houses are too hot in summer and too cold in winter. No longer able to till the rich soil along the Nile, they must try to irrigate the desert.

Tourists leaving the Temple of Horus, Idfu.

"We lived about halfway between Aswan and Abu Simbel," Abdelkadir Mohammed Fadl, an elderly Nubian, told me. "In Korta we had sheep and goats, and in the rich land along the Nile we grew peanuts and vegetables and fruit, and of course dates. We had so many dates then, and they made us rich! Here there are no palms. This is Arab land, not ours. The old land was worth more than gold. This is like aluminum."

I spent several days in one of the relocation villages. In the mornings, I climbed down from my roof tent and visited with the elderly men and women who sat on their stoops, soaking up the warmth of the early sun. In the evenings, I often wrote in my journal in Abdelkadir's sitting room. A gaggle of children crowded around, staring over my shoulder. One evening when the television was on, the children could not decide whether to watch it or me. Every five seconds their heads swung back and forth between the Egyptian soap opera and the *khawajah* (foreigner) sitting live in their house.

Not many young men live in the village. Since the loss of their farms, most of them seek employment in Saudi Arabia and other oil-rich Arab states. The televisions, radios, and other goods in the village were evidence of money the men send home, but they are separated from their families for ten months a year.

The Nubians will probably never go back to their land. It would take an enormous amount of money, which the government does not have, to reclaim bits of the desert along the shores of Lake Nasser. And the Nubians would be reluctant to give up the schools, clinics, electricity, and roads of which they have grown fond during the last 20 years. Many people told me they could not understand why the international community pitched in $40 million to save the ancient temples at Abu Simbel, but were not concerned about the people.

"We left our fathers and our grandfathers in the ground there at Korta, and they are lost. We are sad to lose them," Abdelkadir explained. "There is no more time of sitting in the shade of the date palm, of drinking from the Nile."

"And what about the children?" another man asked. "The father can tell his children about the old land, but it is different to see it, to hear the palms in the wind, to bathe in the Nile. We have young people who are 20 years old and never have they seen their own land. They never will."

"How can they know the old ways? Before, all the things we learned from our fathers were still there," Abdelkadir went on. "When a couple was getting married, people came from all over, and there was a big festival for seven days to celebrate. Now people are getting married in only one day. And a funeral that was fifteen days is now just only two."

I asked Abdelkadir why he thought it had changed so much.

"Civilization," he replied. "There is no time for festivals here. This world is in a hurry."

ASWAN IS the end of the line. It is the southern terminus of the road and railway from Cairo, the turnaround for luxury ships. Just as the first cataract cut ancient Egypt off from Nubia, the High Dam now separates the Nile Valley from over 300 miles of virtually uninhabited desert and lakeshore that stretch to the Sudan border and beyond. Aswan is now, as it was then, the end of Egypt proper.

Aswan was all blue and gold; the sand of the western desert plunged right down into the river that reflected the azure sky. The air was light and dry, neither hot nor cold, and the atmosphere more relaxed than at Luxor. White-sailed *feluccas* ferried tourists between Elephantine Island, the tombs of the governors of Aswan, Plantation Island, and St. Simeon's monastery.

Detail of the statue of Ramses II, Luxor Temple.

I checked into a breezy room at the Old Cataract Hotel for a few days before I caught the boat that sails from Aswan across Lake Nasser. The government would not let anyone drive across the desert, and the weekly boat was the only way to Sudan. I wanted to take advantage of the clean sheets and hot showers, the last of tourist comforts.

I tried desperately to get a photograph of the High Dam, but could not. The man assigned by the information office to help me was nice enough, but he spoke no English, and we communicated in fractured French. I do not think it really mattered. The High Dam is simply a stone wall, 364 feet high, 12,565 feet long at the crest. It could only be decently photographed from the air, and for security reasons no one is allowed to fly near it.

On the last day in Aswan, I changed the car's oil and filters and filled the tank and jerry cans with 120 gallons of diesel; there would be no more fuel (or roads or hotels) until I reached Khartoum a month later. Then I drove to the dock and onto the boat that sails across the lake.

The boat was actually three vessels: the boat itself with crew quarters and first-class cabins, and two open-decked barges lashed to the sides. On the barges the 600 or so third-class passengers spread their mats, stashed their bundles of wares, and settled down for the 40-hour voyage. I stowed my car on the lower deck of one of the barges, after considerable maneuvering and not a little concern that the wooden gangplanks would give under the weight.

At dawn the first morning, it looked as if the decks were covered with heaps of white cloth. As they stirred, though, I realized the lumps were people huddled beneath their robes. Slowly they awoke and set about their routines, facing east for morning prayers and dipping water from the lake to make tea over charcoal fires.

Villagers in a tea house, El Araba.

I sipped my tea in the spacious comfort of the galley, staring through the windows at the crowd on the barge about three feet away. It was like a Buñuel film. But that is Africa: a tiny elite live in luxury, everybody else subsists. The economic distance is enormous, the physical distance often quite small.

I spent the day talking with the men on one of the barges (there were very few women on board), doing my best with the little Arabic I know, they doing their best with English. The conversations were not complex, but we were trying so hard that the attempt became the communication, and in a way was more important than any particular thing we might have said.

I learned that the men were Sudanese. They drive camels to Egypt, where they bring high prices "because the Egyptians like to eat them." With the money they buy inexpensive manufactured goods to take home to sell. The deck was covered with bundles of towels, plastic shoes, tin pots, and kettles.

At one point I checked on my car. People were camped around and on it, but that was not what worried me. Several men had built fires up against the car, which made a good windbreak. It also contained over a hundred gallons of fuel. I protested to the men, but my caution meant very little to them. "Malesh" (never mind), they said. (A few months later on a similar boat, 300 people died when a cooking fire ignited drums of fuel. The steamer caught fire and sank.)

We slipped through the turquoise lake, with no sound but the gentle throb of the engine and the swoosh of water against the three hulls. The western desert was completely flat, but to the east, jagged, dark hills jutted up from the sand. We passed only a few scattered fishermen's huts, and during the second night the town of Abu Simbel, where the famous temples were relocated. There was no other sign of life.

As I left Egypt, I was caught once again between images of its past and the reality of its present. Sailing across the new lake, I thought only about what lay beneath. I must have passed over Abdelkadir's home, and his fields, and his date trees, and the father and grandfather he was sad to have lost.

Nubian girl and grandmother, Korta Talit.

Cairo.

Fishermen rowing past a houseboat, on Cairo's "Little Nile" between Zemalek Island and Giza.

Mosque of Ahmad ibn Tulun, Cairo.

Street scene, old Cairo.

Pyramids from Mena House Oberoi, former guest house of the Khedive Ismail, Giza.

Mud house painted with the name Allah, south of Cairo.

Ramesseum and Colossi of Memnon, Nile Valley, Luxor.

Temple to Sobek, the crocodile deity, and Harwer, the falcon deity, Kom Ombo.

Detail of pillars, Kom Ombo.

33

Woman rowing, Damietta.

Felucca on the Nile, Aswan.

Old Cataract Hotel, Aswan.

Tomb of Tutankhamun in the Valley of the Kings, west bank of Luxor.

Mortuary temple of Queen Hatshepsut, Deir el Bahri, west bank of Luxor.

Painting inside Sennedjem's tomb, Deir el Medina, west bank of Luxor.

Remains of an ancient wall overlooking the Nile, Kom Ombo.

41

Temple of Ramses II, Abu Simbel.

NORTHERN SUDAN

When the boat pulled into Wadi Halfa at the end of the voyage across Lake Nasser, the differences between Egypt and Sudan were immediately apparent. I saw no docks, no customs and immigration offices, no structures of any sort—just a rocky spot where the steamer pulled close enough for its gangplanks to reach the shore. A vague track led across loose sand to what there was of the new town. Old Wadi Halfa had been drowned by the lake, which extends 100 miles into Sudan, and is here called Lake Nubia.

In some ways northern Sudan mirrors Egypt; Nubians live nearest the lake, Arabs inhabit the reach from Dongola to Khartoum. The means of existence, too, is the same; people cultivate the alluvial banks of the Nile. Like their Egyptian relations, many Sudanese Nubians saw their homes and farms inundated; 34,000 of them were relocated to an irrigated project called New Halfa, 800 miles from the Nile. Those beyond the lake's reach got none of the benefits from the dam; there is neither electricity to light their homes and pump water to their fields, nor perennial irrigation to increase their income. About 15,000 showed the spirit that has enabled Nubians to hold onto their language and culture in the face of thousands of years of Egyptian and Arab invasion—they refused to move.

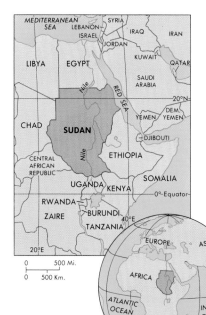

It took all day to disembark. We arrived at 8:00 a.m., but every bundle on board had to be checked, and it was 5:00 p.m. when I drove off the barge. I was learning, willy-nilly, to slow down to Sudan's pace. The customs officer, Kamal Hassan Osman, looked over my car and camera gear, and eventually stamped my papers. Then he invited me to his home.

Kamal's house, like the others in town, was new. Its large courtyard and rooms were surrounded by a six-foot adobe wall, the same reddish brown as the desert. The mayor, Mohammed Ahmed Deram, came to meet the stranger in town, and the three of us sat outside Kamal's compound, sipping tea and goat's milk. The story I heard was much the same as the Egyptian Nubians', but with a twist.

"The government came here to make people move," Kamal told me. "But we preferred to stay in our own land. When we refused to move, the government treated us like outlaws. Some people were imprisoned; those who worked for the government lost their jobs."

"They closed the schools, the hospital, stopped these boats coming from Aswan, and threatened to take out the railroad that goes from here to Khartoum," the

(Facing) Rashaida mother and child, near Suakin.

mayor said. "But we Nubians got together. Nubian teachers and doctors came back here and worked for no pay. We put our money together and bought two big trucks that could bring us food.

"Fortunately, that government did not have time to finish with us. In 1969, they were overthrown. We held out, and the new government started to help us. But it is difficult. The land away from the river is not good, and irrigation is too expensive. We did not even get electricity from that dam that forced us to move. We are trying to learn to fish in the lake, but it is not our custom, and it will take time to learn this new way of life."

"The people who moved to New Halfa want to come back," Mohammed explained. "But how can they survive here when even we few are finding it hard? They are suffering from malaria and the social life there. They may be gaining from the wheat and cotton they grow, but you know, getting money is not the only thing. They live a long way distant, and they never see their relations anymore.

"In New Halfa the old customs are finished. All the people are speaking Arabic, and the young ones do not know their own place. Even here it is spoiled now because we have lost the environment of the Nubian way of life; we have lost the Nile."

The next morning Kamal introduced me to his mother, Fatima Abdu Mahmoud, and his grandmother, Hamida Mohammed Ibrahim. Both women wore long black dresses and black *tobes* draped over their heads and shoulders. Fatima sat on one of the three beds that lined the walls of the windowless room. Hamida sat on the earthen floor, leaning against her daughter's legs and worrying a string of pearl-

Washing dust and sand from a bus engine, Nile, near Khartoum.

smooth and radiant beads. She reckoned that she was about 80 years old, though did not know for sure. The hot sun and dry air of Nubia had etched deep creases in her face. Cataracts clouded her eyes, but her voice was strong and certain.

"When I was young, the Valley was full of Nubian people, all of them relatives with no foreigners living in between. My father had a big farm with wheat and many kinds of vegetables, and very many date palms. I used to help him working in the fields and bringing water from the Nile. Everything was very nice; life was pleasant. We used to sit in the shade of the palms, and I would listen to the stories.

"I was married when I was young — about 15, I think. On the second night of the marriage, my husband and I went to the Nile at 4:00 in the morning and washed each other's faces in the water of the river and drank from the Nile. This was the Nubian custom, you see.

"When I was a girl, before the time when I was married, some of the young men thought I was beautiful; they used to call me 'Shamandura,' which means

'the light that shines on the river at night to guide the boats.' But if there is no river, how can there be Shamandura?"

THE MAIN WAY out of Wadi Halfa follows the railway line southeast across the desert to meet the Nile at Abu Hamed, 230 miles away. I drove along the great loop of the Nile, 540 miles to reach the same point. Only occasionally do trucks use the Nile route, and they leave a confusing trail. Drivers avoid the ruts left by previous vehicles, so myriad tracks fan out over miles of desert, frequently disappearing altogether, obscured by blowing sand. All I could do was pick out one set of tracks, hope whoever made them was going the same place I wanted to, and pray that he had gotten there.

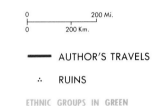

In Egypt I had grown used to paved roads, gas stations, hotels, and even to the crowds. I was seldom alone there, and though it was irritating at times, it was also comforting; people were always nearby in case anything went wrong. Now I was heading into uninhabited desert.

The very difficulty of travel is what makes places like northern Sudan so worth the visit. In Egypt, guidebook in hand, I had basically gone from A to B, defining my journey by the check list. Sudan, the size of the United States east of the Mississippi, has no guidebooks, mostly because there are no roads down which to be guided.

Rivers of golden sand flowed between islands of harsh, brittle rock. The trick was to get up enough speed descending one island to make it through the soft sand to the next. The north wind blew dust raised by my tires in through the windows, coating me and everything inside the car. It was slow going: four-wheel drive, first and second gear.

I was driving a Mercedes 300GD, a five-cylinder diesel. When I left Wadi Halfa, it was weighed down with 120 gallons of fuel, 20 gallons of water, a tool box, spare parts, canned food, extra tires, several boxes of camera gear, a few shirts and pants, a roof tent, and, strapped on the back, a 185cc motorcycle.

The car was my home for most of eight months, and except for food I carried everything I might possibly need for my drive up the Nile. If I ran out of anything, the markets along the way were unlikely to provide it. When I lost my one pair of shoes, even the shops in Sudan's capital proved inadequate; I bought the biggest sneakers I could find and still had to cut out the toes.

The Mercedes had been outfitted at the factory in Stuttgart. The rear seats were removed to make room for my gear. A foam-rubber lined, lockable metal box within easy reach behind the passenger's seat protected my cameras and lenses, more from jostling and dust than from thieves. A shelf divided the rest of the back; jerry cans below, clothes, food, etc., above. A water can mounted on the roof was my solar shower. (The water was often too hot. I had to paint the can white.)

The roof tent has to be one of the best pieces of safari gear ever invented. Mine was a box, hinged at one end so that the ribs and fabric formed an arc as it unfolded. Half of the tent stuck out over the rear of the car, creating some shade to sit in; a telescoping ladder provided access.

I slept in villages or in the desert, depending on where I happened to be when it got dark. I never needed to clear thorns and stones out of the way, and it was nice to be up in the air, for the cooling breezes and because it put me beyond the reach of snakes and scorpions and, farther south, lions and hyenas.

Northern Sudanese women, Jebel Barkal.

I did not travel far the first day. *Malesh.* I was not about to drive through the desert at night, and with several hundred square miles to myself, there was no need to look for a campsite. In late afternoon I just stopped. I quickly grew accustomed to the desert's solitude, and found it refreshing after months in Egypt. I heard no sound, just the deep silence I have only felt in true desert, where there is nothing to stir but the rocks and sand.

I clambered up one of the high, crumbly hills nearby. No pollution, no lights, not even moisture sullied the air; in the soft, late light the sky had a depth that pulled at my eyes. The desert stretched east 400 miles to the Red Sea, west 3,000 miles to the Atlantic Ocean. The Nile is a linear oasis, a living thread of blue and green sewn across the wasteland.

THE NEXT AFTERNOON I saw, for the first time, the natural, undammed, unfettered Nile as it came into view from a ridge overlooking the village of Akasha. Here Nile Valley people lived as they had before the High Dam: the fields of the Nubians in Akasha were each year flooded and coated with silt, and they still had the date trees so mourned in Kom Ombo and Wadi Halfa.

"Those people who lived to the north lost all their fields and houses," Hassan Mohammed Salih, a local school teacher, told me. "But by the will of Allah this is where the lake stopped. Here we could keep our old land."

Hassan led me through the fields. Men gathered up their white, pale green, or blue *gellabiahs* and crouched to tend earthen dams in fields of onions and tomatoes. Some climbed the female date palms to fertilize them with pollen. Six months later, Hassan told me, they would climb them again to harvest the dates.

Barefooted women squatted in the bean fields, beating dry pods with sticks to free the beans, then winnowing them in the breeze that rustled their diaphanous *tobes*. They giggled when, stopping to watch them, I greeted them in Nubian, "Maskajiro." According to Hassan, the women and older children speak only Nubian; men learn Arabic for business dealings and travel. But the younger children are beginning to learn Arabic because the new school is taught in that language. Nubian has no script.

In the evening we sat on a straw mat eating dates, leaning against the wall of Hassan's compound, our backs to the flinty hills that rose on the desert's edge. Donkeys laden with the day's harvest were driven past by people who paused briefly to greet us, then pushed on toward cooking smells from compounds nearby. All the men said the same thing to me: "Akasha kwais," which can mean either "How do you like Akasha?" or "Akasha is good."

"This place is very good," Hassan said. "Without the Nile there is no life, nothing! You can see the rich earth the Nile brings to us. We grow plenty of wheat and beans and

Schoolroom, Belel, across the Nile from Karima.

vegetables for our food. And we have goats and sheep for milk and meat. Ah, and the dates. They bring us money, and we use everything from them. Our houses are made from the mud and sand of the Nile, which we mix with colors from the desert. Then we cut the trunk of the palm to make the roofs, which are covered with the fronds. We have all that we need here."

His easy contentment reminded me of the people in the Egyptian Delta. Like them, the Nubians in Akasha had not been affected by the Aswan High Dam. The lives of both are beyond its long reach.

THE CHALLENGING THING about driving through Nubia was to keep moving. I stopped often to walk along the river, watching people at work in the fields. Everywhere they invited me into their homes for tea or food. Even when I was just driving through a village — slowly, so as not to raise too much dust — people tried to be hospitable. Children came pouring out of the houses and ran beside the car, yelling, "Stop, stop." It was the only English they knew. When I did, a few of them would disappear into a house and re-emerge seconds later, bashfully thrusting a dish of dates at me. When I did not stop, I felt unfriendly. But it would have taken me years to reach Khartoum.

When I rode the ferry to Dongola (no bridges cross the Nile in the 1,092 miles between Aswan and Khartoum), I passed from Nubian land into Arab. The term "Arab" refers to most of the people in northern Sudan; Arab tribes, migrating into Sudan from Egypt and across the Red Sea, took over that part of the country in the 14th and 15th centuries. They displaced many of the indigenous peoples and absorbed others. Some Arab tribes remained nomadic and spread out across the breadth of Sudan, through the region where true desert gives way to seasonally habitable semidesert. Others settled in the Nile Valley between Dongola and Khartoum.

(Above and facing) Three generations of Kababish nomads, northern Kordofan.

South of Dongola, the western desert was quite different from the eastern one; instead of alternating rivers of sand and islands of rock, there were endless dunes. In the early mornings, the sand was firm, but it loosened with the heat and by afternoon pulled at the car. Whenever I got stuck, the heavy car quickly sank up to its axles, and I had to get out the shovel, dig out the sand, haul the aluminum sand ladders down from the roof, and put them in front of the wheels. Usually the little momentum was enough to get me going again. But what about the sand ladders I left behind? I drove around in circles looking for a firm spot to stop, always, it seemed, quite some distance. Then I slogged through the sand and dragged the ladders back to the car. I did this more times than I would care to admit before realizing that I needed only to tie a rope to the ladders and pull them along.

The heat was oppressive — well over 100° F. I had decided against getting air conditioning in the car, thinking it would suck power from the engine, and that it would be better for me to become accustomed to the heat. I had also been afraid that, seduced by the comfort, I would never get out of the car, but take all the photographs through the window and invite people inside to talk rather than visit them in their homes.

Shade was rare. Inside the car was like a furnace, which made me worry about the film — stored in cold boxes with nothing to keep them cold. I had noticed that the water hanging in goatskins on the sides of nomads' camels was always cool. Evaporation! Not having any goatskins to stuff my film into, I wrapped wet towels around the boxes.

Because of heat, dust, and the time I spent crawling around in muddy fields or digging sand out from underneath the car, I needed to do laundry every few days. Water, soap, and dirty clothes went into a sealed bucket in the very back of the car, the bounciest place. The agitation, as I drove over the rough tracks and lurched through the sand, was terrific. After a while I stopped, changed the water, and rinsed. At night I draped my clean clothes over the car to dry.

Across from Karima, I drove down to the Nile to ask about the ferry. An old man sitting at the landing said that the ferry would run "Bukra inshallah" (To-morrow, God willing). The man, Mohammed Alhassan Mansour, made me promise to sleep at his house that night, and waited for me while I bathed in the Nile.

The farms along this stretch of the Nile were different from those farther north with their fields of wheat, alfalfa, and beans. Here orchards of mangos, citrus, and the ubiquitous date palms stretched half a mile from the Nile. Nestled among them were the familiar walled houses.

Mohammed and I sat on the long verandah in front of his sitting room, smiling at each other; after an exchange of pleasantries, there was not much we could say. *Malesh.* He disappeared into the room and emerged with an enormous boom box. "You like BBC?" he asked as he tuned the radio to the British Broad-casting Corporation. It did not matter that he could not understand a word of the English soccer match. I was his guest.

Abdulahi, Mohammed's young nephew who had learned some English in school, joined us. He and I practiced our vocabulary on each other, pointing to what-ever happened to be around and saying our respective words. Soon Mohammed's two wives brought large trays laden with dinner—goat and mutton stews, tomato and okra dishes, and *kissra*, a thin bread used to pick up the sauces.

I never quite got used to the separation of the sexes during my travels in Arabic areas. While not as severe as in Arabia, it was nonetheless disconcerting. In the fields and markets there seemed to be an easy exchange between men and women, but whenever I was in someone's home, I saw women only when they brought tea or food, after which they disappeared until the men finished eating. They could then eat, in the kitchen, what was left.

I realize that I missed a lot because my contact was limited to men, but there was little I could do. I could usually find men who spoke English, but women rarely knew a second language. When I did talk with them, it was always a formal ex-change through a translator. As soon as the interview was over, I was led back to where men were supposed to spend their time.

That night I unfolded my roof tent outside Mohammed's compound and wrote in my journal for a while, looking through the tent flap at a full moon rising behind the rustling palm trees and glimmering on the glassy surface of the Nile. I went to sleep early, but not for long. My journal from the next day reads:

"Felt as if I were about to buy the farm last night. Had felt a little ropey when I went to bed, but didn't think much of it. Woke up at 11:30 with ter-rible chills, body shaking, head splitting. Didn't feel like food poisoning—know that one far too well—but maybe.

"Climbed down, took some tetracycline, vitamins, aspirin, swallowed with vitamin C. Woke up again at 1:00 extremely thirsty and still chilled. Body unbelievably hot. Again at 4:00, drenched with sweat.

"Today chills gone but horrible headache and weak. Wonder what it is? Thought of all the things I did yesterday — ate liver and *ful* (beans) for breakfast, drank water in Korti, had dinner at Mohammed's, a bath in the Nile, have an acacia thorn embedded in my foot. Malaria — new or recurrent? Just don't know. I hate this self-diagnosis and treatment. Nearest hospital in Khartoum, and that might be worse than none. Swallow pills and hope."

My illness turned out not to be serious, and I was fine after a couple of days. But this was not the only, or the worst, incident. On this sort of journey, I try not to let myself think about possible disasters, or the number of days it might take to get to a medical facility. I do what I can to minimize the risks, then accept them, shrug, and dive in.

Siphons irrigating sugar fields, Kenana.

What goes into my mouth is a particular problem. I have eaten all sorts of things during my travels, not because I wanted to, but because to refuse food is a terrible insult. Often, when someone fed me, it meant that his family would not have enough, or that my host, having borrowed some chickens or home-brew from a neighbor, would be in debt for months. The custom is to honor a traveler with food, and so bring honor to your household. Some food, like the stuffed squab in northern Sudan, is delicious. Camel and hippopotamus stews taste fine. Some of it, though, like curdled milk and ox blood, is hard to swallow. Other dishes are hard even to look at; I was once proudly presented with a large bowl of monkey stew and urged to pick out one of the fingers by its tiny fingernail.

JUST SOUTH of Karima, a hill, Jebel Barkal, rises above the desert. Called Napata in ancient times, the place was the capital of an indigenous dynasty, the Kingdom of Kush which arose in the eighth century B.C. Its powerful monarchs extended their realm into Egypt, where they ruled as the pharaohs of the XXV Dynasty. Their reign in Egypt was brief, but flourished at Napata until 300 B.C., when the capital was moved farther up the Nile to Meroe.

The ruins of the temple of Amon lie at the foot of Jebel Barkal. Bits and pieces of walls, floors, columns, and statues protrude from the sand like litter on a windswept beach. Nearby, a field of pyramids quietly crumbles into the desert. There are no signs, admission fees, or fences, no tour buses or touts. The antiquities of Kush have not attracted tourists or many archaeologists, and impoverished Sudan cannot afford to investigate its past. The needs of the present are too pressing.

I had driven northeast to reach Karima, following the great S the Nile carves into the Nubian Desert. As I continued in that direction toward Abu Hamed, the character of the land changed. The adobe houses vanished, replaced by occasional straw-mat huts of nomads who water their flocks of sheep and goats in the Nile. A few bushes and stands of coarse grass clung to the dunes, the only sign of vegetation I could see. One day some goats wandered near my campsite, licking between the stones and sand. I could not imagine what they found there to eat.

At dawn my thermometer recorded 80° F. Noon was unbearable; not a breath of wind stirred, and the sun reflected off the desert in a white, shimmering heat. (I have a note in my journal about burning my lips when melted ChapStick poured out of its tube.)

I was faced with a dilemma. Driving in the midday heat was gruelling. But waiting out the middle of the day was worse; there was no shade, and it was excruciatingly boring. I read and reread the few books I had and grew tired of my dozen tapes. My journal is full of heat- and boredom-induced ramblings which do little but fill up pages. I usually drove.

I had my routines. Getting unstuck and fixing flat tires were sometimes part of them. To break the monotony, I did laundry and moistened the towels protecting my film. In the evenings I bathed in the Nile or showered from the water can on the roof of the car. I drank lots of water, opened a can of herring or something equally salty, and added more salt. I drank tea, ate whatever canned fruit had the most juice, drank some more boiled water from the Nile. I rarely urinated. I was sweating buckets, but never realized it because evaporation was instantaneous. I got salt poisoning (which, despite its name, comes from a lack of salt). I listened to the BBC, but the headlines and falling dollar did not mean a whole lot. I crawled up into the roof tent and went to sleep — at about 8:30.

Irrigated fields on the bank of the Nile, Omdurman.

Sometimes there was a howling wind, a sandstorm, a *haboob*. I would wake up in the night with the tent shaking violently and full of sand. In the daytime *haboobs* reduced visibility to almost nothing.

At Abu Hamed I rounded the loop of the Nile, met up with the railway line and track from Wadi Halfa, and turned south, pushing on to the town of Atbara where the river of that name flows into the Nile. During its flood, the Atbara contributes 22 percent of the Nile's volume. This seasonal input is the only water the Nile gets between Khartoum and the Mediterranean, a distance of 1,900 miles through one of the world's fiercest deserts.

But by the time I got to Atbara I was not interested in all this. I went straight to the market and there, among the sheep and goat carcasses, the beans, tomatoes, okra, and spices, the cheap manufactured goods I had seen on the boat crossing

Lake Nasser, I found one thing I was desperately looking for, salt tablets, and something of which I had not even dared dream—ice.

UPSTREAM FROM ATBARA, on the east bank of the Nile, lies Meroe, the site to which the Kings of Kush moved their capital after abandoning Napata. The empire flourished at Meroe until the fourth century A.D., when an invasion by the Abyssinian Kingdom of Axum put an end to Kush. The Meroitic script on the walls of the temples, tombs, and pyramids was based on the Egyptian, but evolved in isolation and has yet to be deciphered.

Nubian compound, Akasha.

Farther south, and much farther out into the eastern desert, lie two other Meroitic sites, Naqa and Musawwarat, the latter a large temple complex set deep in a valley. It, like the ruins at Jebel Barkal, is a broken, sand-swept jumble. The *gafir* (guard) and his children were thrilled to have a visitor, and we had a pleasant time roaming the ruins. Then we piled into my car to drive to the *gafir's* house for tea. Only later that night did I realize he had taken my one pair of shoes, leaving me only with flip-flops.

I camped near a well used by Birbanega nomads. Away from the Nile, water is precious and deep in the ground. It was drawn from the 120-foot well in goatskin bags tied to one end of a rope, the other end of which was attached to a pair of donkeys driven down the slope. A wide circle of the land around the well had long been overgrazed, so the people were obliged to camp about two hours away. Every day they trekked to the well, drew water, loaded it on their animals, and carried it home.

Nearing the end of this leg of my journey, I became concerned about running low on fuel and endurance. A month of heat, dust, and rough tracks was taking its toll. In my journal the next day, I wrote:

"Drove along, suddenly realizing I was going to be in Khartoum. Then pavement. Traffic—cars, buses, taxis, trucks. Had to remember to stay to one side of the road. Road!

"To the Hilton, at the confluence of the Blue and White Niles ('Longest kiss in history'—Arabic poetry). Lots of Mercedes waiting to take their owners to dinner, lobby full of well-dressed businessmen in suits and brilliantly white, flowing *gellabiahs.* I look terrible. Filthy, unshaven, gritty face streaked with sweat. People look at me funny. Luckily some of the staff remember me from earlier travels, warm welcome. More luckily, they had a room. Mail waiting.

"Got the stuff out of the car and into the room. Air conditioning! Ordered beers from room service [this was shortly before Islamic law made alcohol illegal in Sudan]. Drew a bath and lay in it drinking cold beer, reading the mail. Heaven."

Pyramids from the Kingdom of Kush, Jebel Barkal.

Kawahla man herding sheep and goats to water, Edit Moya.

Village in the dry hills, north of Meroe ruins.

Kababish man and his donkeys traveling in a haboob *(sandstorm), near Hamrat el Wuz.*

Hamida Mohammed Ibrahim and her granddaughter, Wadi Halfa.

Man fetching water to wash himself before entering the mosque of Mohammed Alhassal Eljibalia, Kassala.

Passengers pushing a bus stuck on its 240-mile trip from Dongola to Khartoum.

Mosque of the Mahdi, Omdurman.

64

Shopkeeper, Omdurman.

People climbing sand slope of Jebel Barkal.

ETHIOPIA

*K*hartoum stands at the confluence of the two branches of the Nile. The White Nile, the great, steady parent stream, begins 2,260 miles to the south, deep in the heart of Africa. The Blue Nile originates 852 miles to the southeast, at Lake Tana in the highlands of Ethiopia. Torrential rains there cause the floods that sweep down to Khartoum and on toward Egypt. At flood time, the Blue Nile contributes 70 percent of the Nile's waters, the rest of the year only 20.

The failure of those rains was largely responsible for the 1984 Ethiopian famine that made world headlines and stirred the hearts of people everywhere. I was in Ethiopia two years earlier, and so that disaster plays no part in this account. Nor will I delve deeply into politics: both Haile Selassie's antiquated feudal regime and Mengistu Haile Mariam's Marxist regime are beyond the scope of this book. My impression of Ethiopia's political situation was that one repressive, dogmatic, and intolerant form of government has been replaced by another. As one Ethiopian put it, "There is no question that Ethiopia needed a revolution. We're still waiting for it."

Moving around in Ethiopia was even more difficult than it had been in northern Sudan, but for entirely different reasons. There are plenty of good roads—the problem was getting permission to drive on them. Every trip outside the capital region required a special pass from the Ministry of Security, which the officials were reluctant to issue. Ethiopia had been mostly closed to western journalists since the 1974 revolution, and, in 1982, the authorities were suspicious of an American who wanted to go everywhere, talk to everybody, and photograph everything. They were convinced I was a spy.

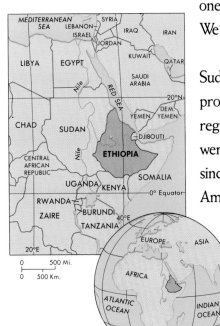

It took me several months to get an entrance visa, and, once I was there, another three weeks to get permission to leave Addis Ababa. At the end of each trip to the countryside, I went back to Addis to work on the next permit. In Ethiopia, the usual bureaucratic inefficiencies were compounded by an astonishing degree of rear-end covering. Nobody wanted to be held responsible for letting me do anything.

I was not allowed to drive myself to the specified places. Instead I had to rent a car with a driver and a "minder." I was lucky that the one I got understood what I was trying to do, was helpful, and a good companion. I needed an inter-

(Facing) Afar nomad girl, Sampati.

preter in any case. But I was always concerned that the people with whom I was talking might not be completely honest, since they were speaking through someone from the government. When, for example, I asked one farmer if his life was better than it had been before the revolution, he looked at the government man and told me, "The government says it is better."

I spent two months traveling south, east, and west of Addis in the parts most recently incorporated into the empire of the Christian Amhara people of the central highlands, and where the feudal system was most onerous. In the wake of conquest, land was divided among the church, favorites of the crown, and soldiers of the victorious army. Reduced to landless peasants, the local inhabitants were compelled to turn over from one-half to two-thirds of their crops to absentee landlords. Schools and hospitals served only the urban elite. At the time of the 1974 revolution, the illiteracy rate was 93 percent and life expectancy was 39 years.

In the southern and western provinces, people spoke of great changes in their lives. Mostly the changes related to the extension of public services, but there was also a sense, for the first time, of being part of the country.

"I used to think that reading and writing were something magic, something that was only a gift for people of high birth," one woman told me. "When I was a girl there were no schools. The things that were real for me were growing crops, fetching water and firewood, and getting married when I was 15. Beyond that there was nothing."

The literacy campaign launched by the new government was indisputably a good thing, and land reform was long overdue. But the policy of forced resettlement caused undue hardship. Moving people into centralized villages made the provision of services easier. It also made people easier to control. Since farmers were expected to till the same land as before, many spent several unproductive hours each day walking between house and field. Even if they managed to grow more crops than their families required, they were forced to sell the excess to the government at a price less than the cost of production.

Women fetching water in gourds beside a tanqua *(reed boat), Lake Tana.*

These resettlement programs, along with grossly inefficient state farms, were responsible for a considerable loss of agricultural productivity in a country that should have the production of food as its number one priority. Even two years before the famine, I saw tons of food donated by the West being distributed in areas where soil fertility and rainfall were not problems.

When I drove north of Addis into the heart of the ancient Christian Amhara kingdom, the Abyssinia of old, evidence of the revolution was harder to discern.

I saw few of the posters of Marx, Lenin, and Engels (to whom some Ethiopians referred sarcastically as the "new Trinity") and portraits of Mengistu that abounded in other regions. The revolution had less impact on those whose empire it had been. Land reform, for example, was of little significance; most land in Amhara areas had long been divided into small holdings.

GONDER, IN THE hills north of Lake Tana, was the first permanent capital of the Ethiopian empire, established by Emperor Fasiladas in the 17th century. Before that, the emperors roamed their domain

to keep fractious feudal lords in line. In 1636, Fasiladas built the first of the castles that were to make up Gonder's imperial compound, castles unique on the African continent.

But the castles are historic relics, sitting empty, awaiting the tourists who never come. A more vital part of history are Gonder's 44 churches. The Ethiopian Orthodox Church plays a central role in the lives of the Amharas; it is the very foundation of their culture, their identity, binding the people together through centuries of invasion and isolation.

The *Kebra Negast* (Glory of Kings), written in the 13th century, says that following Christ's rejection by the Jews, the "light of God flew from Israel to the land of Ethiopia, and it shone there with exceeding great brightness, for it willed to dwell there." The notion that Ethiopians are the Chosen Ones is reinforced by the legend of Menelik I, the son of Solomon and Sheba. After visiting Solomon in Jerusalem, the story goes, Menelik returned with the True Ark of the Covenant, containing the stone tablets of the Law. It has remained in Ethiopia ever since, bestowing a special grace on the people.

The wars of conquest by which the Ethiopians spread their empire and religion were seen as battles of light against darkness. The emperor was divine, Chosen of God, descended from the seed of David. His titles included "King of Kings" and "Conquering Lion of the tribe of Judah." But not only the emperor was special. Many Ethiopians told me the following creation story:

"When God was creating man, He first molded him from clay. He put the first batch in the fire, but left them in too long, and they came out burned and black.

71

He threw these away down south. The second batch He took out too soon, and they were pasty white, so He threw them away to the north. The third batch came out just right, and He put them here, in Ethiopia." If Amharas are telling this story to other Ethiopians, they say that God put the third batch in Amhara.

I arrived in Gonder on Good Friday and went to Debre Berhan Selassie (Trinity Church of the Mountain of Light), built in the 1680s. The stone church sits on a

Blue Nile.

hill at the edge of town in a grove of juniper and olive trees, surrounded by a high, fortified stone wall. Unlike the rest of Gonder, it was never destroyed by hostile invaders. It is said that when the Mahdists from Sudan tried to burn the church in 1881, they were attacked and driven off by a swarm of bees.

The Easter Mass started at 8:30 Saturday evening. Many people stayed outside the wall of the church compound, leaning against it or sitting just beyond the gate. Others sat inside the wall, alone or in small clusters beneath the trees; there was no room inside the church. At first I could not figure out why people were segregated. The explanation, when I later heard it, seemed a reflection of the hierarchical nature of the feudal society which had evolved with the church.

The church is centered on the Holy of Holies, where the *tabot,* the representation of the True Ark, is kept. Only priests performing the Mass may enter the Holy of Holies. Around it is the inner sanctum for those who are ritually pure. The rest of the church is for everyone else except those who have not observed the fast, or who have had sexual relations the night before; they must remain outside the wall. The fasting schedule is rigorous. Priests and especially devout people are expected to fast 250 days a year. Ordinary Christians need fast for only 165, including the 48 hours before Easter.

In the light of a single bare bulb, the choir of deacons chanted and beat drums, periodically breaking into gentle, swaying dances. Cloaked all in white—head wraps, robes, *gabes*—they moved like phantoms in the dim hall. Every now and then the music stopped while a priest read from a massive, wood-covered Bible in Ge'ez, the ancient liturgical language from which Amharic is descended. Swinging incense burners filled the church with thick, pungent smoke and sweet aroma. There were no benches or chairs. The floor was covered with a mass of bodies, mostly women and children, some of whom had pulled their *gabes* over them and were sound asleep. I leaned against one of the mud-and-straw plastered walls, feeling drowsy from my two-day fast.

Suddenly the crowd on the floor came to life and rushed at one of the priests handing out lighted tapers; the children almost bowled him over in their enthusiasm to get one of the thin candles before they were gone. As the youngsters retreated to their resting places, the golden glow from a hundred tiny flames spread throughout the church, illuminating the paintings of religious and historical scenes that covered the walls and ceiling.

Preceded by a bell ringer, a priest swinging an incense burner, and another bearing a cross, the *tabot* was carried around the outside of the church three times. The sky was dark and clear; the junipers rustled in the wind. I could not help but feel transported. Medieval European church services must have been much like this. Cut off from the rest of Christianity for centuries after Islam swept the lands around it, the Ethiopian church evolved in isolation. The paintings, the hand-written and illustrated parchment Bibles, the whiff of incense, the steady, slow chants cast a spell of another time, the resonance of which was strangely familiar.

I GOT STUCK in Gonder. My permit from the security authorities expired, and I was not allowed to do anything until a new one arrived from Addis Ababa. The local administrator was extremely unfriendly and opposed to my being there at all. I kept a low profile, not wanting to give him an excuse to throw me out of town, or even worse. I walked the streets and sat around the hotel, waiting—for six days. While browsing in the town's bookstore, I found something to help me pass the time. On a back shelf, covered with dust, was a copy of Evelyn Waugh's *Scoop,* the hilarious satire of journalists working in Abyssinia. Though highly appropriate, it was surprising to find for sale in revolutionary Ethiopia.

When my permit finally arrived, the driver, "minder," and I headed into the Simien Mountains. I was allowed to travel no farther north by road; ongoing guerilla wars in Eritrea, Tigray, and elsewhere made much of the area unsafe.

We drove along the twisting road to the national park headquarters at Sankaber. Looking north, I saw why Ethiopia has historically been difficult to conquer, why the central government has always had trouble maintaining control, and why relief efforts, such as that in 1984, are such a problem. As far as I could see stretched high ridges and vertical-

Ferry crossing Lake Tana.

sided *ambas* (mesas) separated by severe gorges carved over the ages by the rivers that lace the land. The rivers are unnavigable, and during the rainy season most cannot even be forded. The people who scratch livings from the *ambas'* poor soil are a two- or three-day walk from the nearest road.

I hired guides and horses, and with them and a detachment of armed guards, set off along the narrow trail that winds up the mountains. I heard the calls of rare Simien foxes, and occasionally spotted a walia ibex in the distance, standing on a slim ledge cut into a cliff. Only about 300 of this sure-footed antelope remain, all of them high in these mountains.

At some point we passed above the tree line, though I could discern this only by looking closely at the ground vegetation. The land has been occupied for so long by so many people, sheep, and goats that only trees growing in inaccessible gorges survive.

We came out finally onto a vast plain of short, golden grass dotted with 15-foot giant lobelias. At one end of the plain was the village of Geech, a cluster of stone and grass huts surrounded by stingy fields of tilled, rocky earth. People were farming at 12,000 feet.

Sorghum from the United States distributed to Somali nomads in a refugee camp, Jijiga.

I dismounted and wandered among the huts until I came upon Adom Hassan, who was weaving a *gabe* at a loom set up in the lee of a stone wall. His name should have given me a clue that these people were Moslem, but I was in the very heart of Amhara, and assumed everybody would be Christian.

Though Christian and Moslem populations numbered about the same, Moslems were not allowed to own land or hold state office in the empire. Emperor Yohannes the Pious had decreed that all Moslems must live in separate villages or in ghettos. They became merchants and craftsmen, occupations the Amharas considered undesirable.

Adom's ancestors had been converted during an Islamic invasion that overran much of Ethiopia in the 16th century. Most people later reconverted to Christianity, but some, in spite of discrimination, adhered to Islam. A few circumvented the prohibition on owning land by retreating to an altitude at which the Amharas did not want to live. There they set themselves up as farmers, supplementing their meager crops with money earned by weaving cloth for the Christians below.

"We grow barley, potatoes, onions, and ginger," Adom told me. He had invited me into his home to have coffee; three cups, as is the custom, each getting weaker as water is added to the grounds. We sat on three-legged stools around a small fire in the center of the hut. Chakula, Adom's wife, handed me a piece of flat, dry barley bread and a dish of bean stew from the pot that was perched atop three stones surrounding the fire. In language and dress, Adom and Chakula seemed indistinguishable from the Amharas. But religion had been enough to drive them high into the mountains.

"Now is the time for planting, so I am here," Adom went on. "When that is done, I will go to the valley for two or three months to weave for the Abasha (Christians), who bring me spools of thread and pay me to weave it. In this way I can make the money I need to pay taxes and to buy cotton for my family, and sometimes a pot if we need one. When I am there, I live in the house of an Abasha. Whatever grain I get for weaving, I give half to the owner of the house.

"In the past we have fought with the Abasha over this land, but not now. It has not always been easy to be a Moslem in this land."

LEAVING THE Simien Mountains, I found another village that looked the same as the Christian ones, but where, though the people spoke and dressed like the Amharas, religion once again made them outcasts. Known as Falashas (strangers), the people in the village of Bweiteras call themselves Beta Israel; they are the black Jews of Ethiopia. When they became known to the outside world at the turn of this century, the Beta Israel were surprised to learn there were other Jews; they thought they were the only ones. Their continued existence is a testimony to the tenacity with which Ethiopians cling to religion.

Around 1,000 B.C., Sabean Semites from southern Arabia moved into the Ethiopian highlands, importing their more developed culture and intermarrying with the indigenous Agau people. Judaism followed the same path. In the fourth century, when the king at Axum became Christian, most of the people in his expanding empire converted to his religion. Some, mostly small groups isolated in the mountains, refused to give up Judaism. The customs and beliefs of the Beta Israel seem to be largely those transplanted from Arabia long ago.

Somali refugees, Jijiga.

The village resounded. Smiths hammered their wares, potters kneeled over grindstones making powder for their clay. Banned from owning land in 1420, the Beta Israel took up crafts to survive, making themselves necessary to the Amharas but despised and feared because metal working was associated with the "dark crafts." One Amhara told me that as a child he was warned always to run indoors when he saw a Falasha coming, lest he be cursed by the evil eye. The Beta Israel have owned land and farmed since the revolution, but unlike the Moslems, they never really resented being landless.

"Our ancestors came from Jerusalem," a bearded old man named Baynesagn Yainae explained. "The one who led them out of Israel was called Abba Mousie [Moses]. They found themselves in the land of the pharaohs, but were driven into exile. We have lived here ever since. We have no basis to claim land, as we are exiles in this place. We have lived by what we can do with our hands, working metal and making pots for the Christians. It is not bad. We will not always be here.

"We would like to go back to our own land, to Israel," he went on. "And we shall, when it is the will of the God of Israel."

I DROVE OUT of the Simien Mountains back through Gonder and around the eastern shore of Lake Tana to the town of Bahir Dar. From there I set off before dawn in a boat called *Dil Birtigil*. The name means "Victory through Struggle," in keeping with popular revolutionary rhetoric, but was more appropriate than I first realized. The boat was a dilapidated metal clunker, and struggle it did as we chugged slowly out into the lake.

Lake Tana is dotted with 37 islands, and 40 churches and monasteries have been built on them and along the shore. In addition to isolating the monasteries, the islands protected them from Moslem invaders.

We sailed for the monastery of Daga Istephanos, founded in the 13th century on a small, whale-shaped island. The boat landing was at the bottom of a steep slope covered with trees and wild coffee. Mature forests in Ethiopia were always striking—the only big trees I saw were inside church compounds or on sacred islands such as this.

Woman selling kat, *a mild stimulant, to passengers on Addis-Dire Dawa train.*

A monk, Abba Gabriel Tsadik, led us up a long path. Most of the island's 73 monks were working in the fields, and it was quiet around the thatched stone church at the top of the hill. The paintings on the interior mud-and-straw walls were crumbling and fading, and looked as if they would soon be gone altogether.

"People come here at all ages," the monk told me. We were sitting beneath one of the trees, facing the scattered huts where the monks sleep and the glistening water beyond. Abba Gabriel was shy and withdrawn. He would not look at me while we talked, but stared at the ground and fidgeted with his cross.

"Some of us come when very small, some are older men who come here after they have lived normal lives and abandoned that. I myself have been here eight years. I came to join the monastery and was just recently allowed. First I had to study and learn."

In those eight years, Abba Gabriel left the island only one time, to visit another monastery. The monks are largely self-sufficient; they grow enough food for themselves, and the coffee they raise provides cash for whatever few items they require. Their days are spent in prayer and meditation, and in labor in the fields.

"I hope to spend the rest of my life here, in prayer," Abba Gabriel continued. "I do not care for other things, not only the things of the towns, but even the distractions of life in the village. It is good to be away from them. This island has been sacred since antiquity. There have been no females here since then. Because human beings are weak, we must be guarded from temptation. We want to live in purity and chastity here."

I thought he meant female as in women, but the church has a rather more strict interpretation of the word. The prohibition extends to chickens, cows, ewes—the female of any animal.

Just to the east of the church stood a stone building called Beit Elehem, where the sacraments were prepared. Underneath were two rooms, the inner of which contained the remains of several emperors. Abba Gabriel told me how the first one came to be buried there.

"When Fasiladas died, they buried him in Gonder. But every night his voice could be heard crying 'Da.' It made the people very upset, and so they dug him up and carried him all around the country. But every night his voice cried 'Da.' Finally they brought him here. As they carried him up the hill from the water, they had to put him down so they could rest. As soon as he touched the earth the voice said, 'This is it. This is the place where I am to rest.'"

Women at an adult literacy class, Jinka.

ABOUT 18 MILES south of Bahir Dar, the Blue Nile falls 140 feet, beginning its rapid descent from the highlands. I was there at the end of the dry season, and the falls were less full than during the rains, but dramatic nonetheless.

We parked the car at the small village of Tis Abbai, and, after trekking around the falls for a while, went into a little *chai beit* (tea house) to rest before heading back to town. I sat down on a low plank bench across the rough table from a young couple. The woman nestled a small child in her arms and gazed nervously out the door. The man sipped a glass of dark, sweet tea.

I introduced myself to them. The man was Geddif Ashagire (Prop Up and Let Cross), the woman Monyinnet Aynalem (Simplicity is Paradise). Geddif was born where they now live, about half-a-day's walk down the Blue Nile gorge. On their small farm they grew grain and kept beehives, selling the honey to earn money for taxes, clothes, and occasions such as this one. They had come to the village to catch a bus to take their sick child to the hospital.

Geddif and Monyinnet were married when they were about four years old, though they did not live together until she was of age, about 15. They had three other children under ten who were already married, in the old fashion.

I offered them a ride in my car, which Geddif gladly accepted. Monyinnet seemed hesitant. Geddif explained that she had never ridden in a motor vehicle, and had been frightened of the prospect ever since they left home that morning.

It was one of the reasons they were dallying at the tea shop. We finally convinced her that it would be all right. I told the driver to go very slowly, but it did not seem to matter. Poor Monyinnet hid under her *gabe,* and cried the entire way to the hospital.

I have never seen such a look of relief as the one on her face when we stopped, but then two more frightening thoughts seemed to hit her simultaneously: the big town and the masses of people, and the realization that she would have to go through the ordeal all over again to get home. Geddif was torn between comforting his wife and trying to press on me some of the honey he had brought to sell to pay for his child's care.

Anuak farmer shooing birds from a sorghum field, near Itang.

After leaving Geddif and Monyinnet at the hospital, I walked to a spot on the lake shore where the *tanquas* come in from the islands. Most of these reed boats were stacked high with firewood, which brings a good price in the long-deforested area around Bahir Dar. Schoolboys came to the lake in the afternoon to unload the boats, earning as their pay wood to take home for the family fire.

As I walked back to the hotel at dusk, one of the schoolboys caught up with me.

"Good evening," he said. "Welcome to our country."

"Good evening," I replied.

"Where are you from?"

"America."

"Is that a friendly or an imperialist country?"

The boy's remark helped me prepare for my return to Addis, where I arrived for the May Day celebration, heralded in the government-controlled press as a time when "the Ethiopian masses protest against American Imperialism." The masses were at the rally, but not doing a lot of protesting. I later learned that not to attend a rally is to be branded a "counterrevolutionary," and, among other things, to be barred from buying goods at the government stores, where prices are considerably lower than in the market.

The protesting was mostly done by President Mengistu, who reviewed the parades from the same red velvet and gilt chair in which the emperor once sat. Mengistu railed about the "nasty" Americans and the "peace-loving" Soviets who were providing Ethiopia with 2,000 military advisors, 15,000 Cuban troops, and two billion dollars worth of armaments. The Cubans were stationed in the Ogaden region to prevent the Somalis from invading as they had in 1977, when they drove deep into Ethiopia.

The Soviet advisors and most of the armaments were deployed on the northern front. In January, the government had launched the "Red Star Multi-faceted Development Campaign," the desired development being to "wipe out the secessionist bandits" in Eritrea. At the time, it was the latest, but not the first or last, government offensive in a war that has been going on since 1962. There are more than 20 other liberation movements scattered around the country fighting Mengistu's government.

In a complicated superpower shuffle, the Americans and the Soviets switched sides just after the Ethiopian revolution. The Americans had been allies of Ethiopia during Selassie's time, supplying and training his armed forces, with access to facilities there. The Soviets had been friendly with Somalia, and did the same for them. The Somalis, seeking to unify land carved up by Ethiopia, Britain, France, and Italy in 1896, took advantage of the turmoil and confusion in Addis in 1977, and attacked, capturing much of the Ogaden. When the Americans balked at helping repel the invasion, Mengistu appealed to the Soviets who were forced to choose between two bitter enemies. They perceived Ethiopia as the more fertile ground and abandoned Somalia, which promptly tore down the anti-American posters adorning its capital and signed on with the United States.

In some respects, Ethiopia has it both ways. The Soviet Union provides military hardware, but little in terms of economic development and no food. Western-supplied food rescues the people in times of famine, but it also finances a social experiment that is incapable of feeding itself, propping up a government that might fall if it had to survive on its own. There can be no question about feeding starving people. But Mengistu's policies do little to increase food production, and western aid has allowed him to divert money and manpower away from development. As I write this, famine as severe as that of 1984 once again threatens Ethiopia.

Painting of Madonna and child, Debre Berhan Selassie, Gonder.

Mengistu is determined to pursue military solutions to the unwinnable wars that plague his country, and as the fighting drags on, Ethiopia's debt to the Soviets mounts. The Ethiopian Orthodox Church is increasingly under attack. Before my visit, the Abuna (the church patriarch) had been imprisoned and a new one installed by the government. When I wanted to interview the new Abuna, I had to submit a list of written questions long in advance. I was then expected to ask him only those questions, and to believe the prepared answers he read. Since then, the government has attempted to further undermine the church. In order to join the newly formed Communist Party in Ethiopia, Christians, Moslems, and Jews must renounce their religion. For those who are not party members, prospects are dim.

Afar woman securing a bundle to her camel, Sampati.

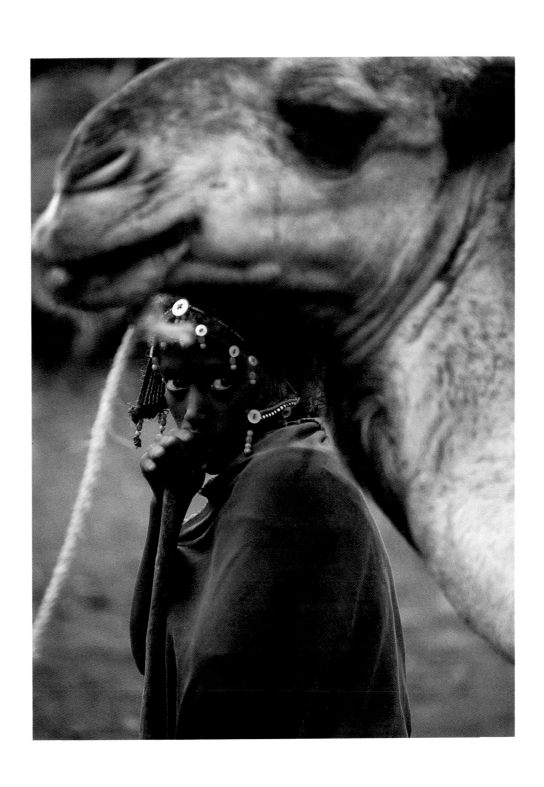

Afar girl with camel, Sampati.

Farmland, near Debre Sina.

Endangered walia ibex, Simien Mountains National Park.

Blue Nile Falls.

Monk, Ntoto Mariam Church, near Addis Ababa.

Beta Giyorgis, Lalibela.

People praying outside church, Asmera.

Monk examining skeleton of Emperor Fasiladas (1632-1667), Monastery of Daga Istephanos, island in Lake Tana.

Narga Selassie Church, Dek Island, Lake Tana.

Anuak dancers singing in praise of the 1974 Revolution, Itang.

Man walking on muddy village road, Afdam.

94

Amhara man and woman outside coffee shop, Debark.

95

Gurage troubadour singing to earn tips in a tea house, Endibir.

Geddif Ashagire, Monnyinet Aynalem, and their child, Tis Abbai.

Oromo woman, Bale region.

SOUTHERN SUDAN

Sudan is a divided country. The numerous northern tribes, united by Islam and the Arabic language, have long dominated the disparate African tribes of the south where, though many are Christians, most people adhere to traditional religions.

In the 19th century, southern Sudan was simply a place northerners raided for ivory and slaves. Northerners came to look upon the Africans as inferiors, and southerners developed an abiding fear and distrust of the Arabs. British administration of Sudan did little to ease the tensions or unify the nation. In 1930, virtually all northerners were forbidden to enter the south. Christian missionaries, on the other hand, were encouraged. The official explanation for the separation was that it protected the southern tribes from being overwhelmed by the north. In reality, it created a human zoo. Railroads, irrigation, and other projects helped the north's economy, but the south remained undeveloped. Consequently, the two regions grew further apart. The few educated southerners had no voice in the talks that preceded independence in 1956. As northern administrators took over southern posts from the British, many southerners felt that it was the dawn of an age of Arab colonialism.

In August 1955, southern army units mutinied and began a civil war that lasted 17 years. The fighting took place in the south, claimed 500,000 lives, and forced another 750,000 to seek refuge in the bush or neighboring countries. The few development efforts there ceased. Southern Sudan was, once again, isolated.

Gaafar Nimeiri came to power in a bloodless coup in 1969, and three years later reached an accord with the southerners granting them regional autonomy. For a while it looked as if the Sudanese had found a way to live together. But the impoverished government in Khartoum could not meet the southerners' raised expectations, and development was slow. The two biggest projects—a pipeline from oil fields in the south to a refinery in the north, and the Jonglei Canal, which would channel Nile water around the Sudd swamp to increase water supplies to northern Sudan and Egypt—were seen as northern exploitation.

Nimeiri added fuel to the fire in 1983 by inexplicably ending southern regional autonomy and imposing *Sharia* law, the Islamic code of justice. Southerners felt

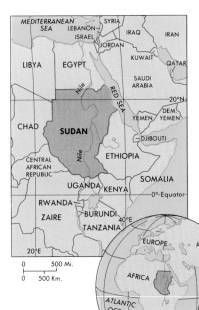

(Facing) Divine King Ayang Anei Kur of the Shilluk, near Fashoda.

betrayed by Nimeiri, whom they had seen as their friend. Relations between the regions once more became tense.

AFTER THE LONG drive from Egypt, I arrived in Khartoum with only four gallons of diesel. I needed enough to reach Uganda, 1,000 miles away, but fuel was rationed in cash-strapped Sudan; to buy more than a few gallons required a permit. I worked through the red tape for three days, then filled up, changed the oil and filters from my stores, and tightened the nuts and bolts that had rattled loose during my drive through the north.

Nubas dancing before the wrestling match, Eluheimir.

I left Khartoum and headed south on a horrendously rough and dusty track. The black cotton soil that makes up the great plain of southern Sudan is cement-hard in the dry season. For almost six months during the rains, the track becomes impassable.

As I drove, sand and rock gave way to soil. Rains fall on this land; life finds sustenance away from the Nile: first scrub, then vast expanses of yellow, eight-foot grass laced with trails revealing the migratory paths of wildlife and cattle. Acacia, palm, and tamarind trees became taller and more deeply green; monkeys played in their branches. Hippopotamus families snorted in the Nile, and at night made their laborious way up the banks to graze. Whenever I stopped, the air was full of bird song, and buzzing insects swarmed to my lantern. I fell asleep listening to the calls of prowling jackals and hyenas.

The people became darker. Fewer men wore *gellabiahs*, women no longer wrapped themselves in *tobes*. The closed, walled compounds of the north gave way to open clusters of thatched, beehive huts.

TO THE WEST of the Nile, about 400 miles south of Khartoum, granite mountains rise to 3,000 feet above the plains. They are the Nuba Mountains, home to the people of that name who live in silo-shaped houses perched among the rocks high above their *dura* (sorghum) fields. Several tribes constitute the Nuba, and they speak languages unrelated to any other African tongue. Their ancestors, members of the ancient Meroitic population, spread throughout northern Sudan and along the Nile, then retreated to the mountains in advance of Arab migrations.

I drove along a track that wound through the hills past fields where women harvested *dura*. The older women wore tattered western dresses. The girls wore beads. Beads decorated their braided hair. Bands of baby-blue beads ran across the hairline to their ears, in front of which hung long, multicolored strands.

Bead chokers adorned their necks, with longer necklaces and bandolier-like beaded strings criss-crossing their bare chests. Wide belts of yellow beads encircled their waists and supported two-inch wide beaded strips that hung down between their buttocks and pieces of leather that shielded their loins. Patterns of small, beadlike scars embellished their torsos and foreheads. Hoops and plugs of gold pierced their ears, noses, and lower lips.

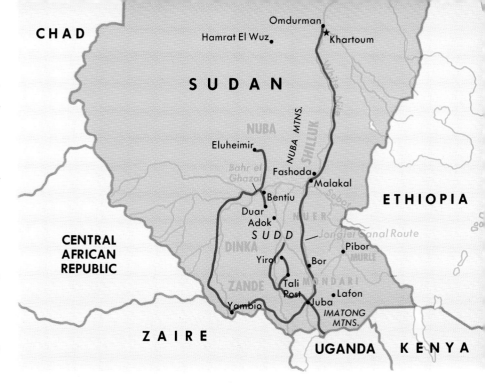

The contrast to the rather homogenous look of the people in northern Sudan and Egypt was striking. The women were unconcerned about my presence. Some walked in from the fields carrying baskets stacked high with the heads of the sorghum plants. Others sorted the heads by color—red, yellow, white—and beat them with long poles.

A group of young men, who were a match for the girls, sat in the shade of a tree beside a seep well. They were dressed in bright, conical hats, Day-Glo shorts, and striped knee socks from which the feet had been cut. Bands of bells adorned their ankles; beaded bracelets were wrapped around their wrists. Many of them wore sunglasses on faces painted white. Their torsos and legs were painted with white geometrical designs.

One of the men played a stringed instrument called a *rababa*, singing and whistling a lilting tune which the others joined for the chorus. I retrieved a small cassette recorder from the car and taped some of the song to play back for them. They were astonished, having never heard themselves recorded before. The girls, with whom they had been flirting, came over to listen and shrieked with laughter.

I had driven into the area just when the celebrations of the *dura* harvest were about to commence. "Bukra fi surra," one man told me. "Tomorrow there is wrestling."

I had no trouble finding the site the next afternoon. Three groups of men representing different tribes gathered in an open field near Eluheimir, a small trading post. Some wore *gellabiahs*, others dressed like the men I saw the day before. Most carried spears or short, small-headed axes. At a signal which I could not perceive, two men from each group put down their weapons, picked up *dura* heads, and walked toward a mound of *dura* in the center of the arena. Upon reaching the pile, they squatted, murmured to each other, and added their offerings. Then they returned to their groups.

The young wrestlers broke into the circle. Two faced off, circling each other slowly. Suddenly one threw his opponent, and a great "whoooooom" went up from the crowd. Then, as swiftly as they had gathered, everybody dispersed.

I did not have a clue to what was going on. I assumed that the pile of *dura* was a prize of some sort, but was surprised when the wrestling was over so fast. Luckily, Farouk, a teenaged boy who knew a little English, adopted me for the next two days, guiding me through Nuba Thanksgiving. This was just the preliminary ceremony, he explained, and everybody had gone home to drink *marissa* (sorghum beer). There would be more wrestling later.

Nuba wrestlers at harvest celebration, Eluheimir.

At about 3:00 that afternoon, people, most of whom carried egg-shaped gourds full of *marissa*, assembled in the field. Sitting in groups, the wrestlers used their axes to dig small notches in the earth to cradle the gourds. More and more people poured in. The drinking got serious.

Dancing began. Older women led the singing, keeping time with bells around their ankles and accompanied by men beating large skin drums. A line formed, dancing follow-the-leader style in a long snake that folded back in on itself, carving a circle out of the mass. When not drinking *marissa* or dancing, the wrestlers strutted about like cocks and occasionally ran short distances with long, loping strides.

The circle cleared. Wrestlers burst into the open space, slapping the ground with V-shaped pieces of leather at the ends of poles, showing themselves off to the audience. A wrestler from one team picked up a handful of dirt and threw it contemptuously at the feet of another. The challenged one kneeled with arms raised and a look of extreme boredom on his face. The challenger swaggered around in front of him yelling, then stood in front of the girls from his tribe, who emboldened him with songs of his prowess. These cheerleaders had smeared oil over their beaded bodies and glistened as they danced and sang.

The match began. The combatants circled each other slowly, grasping for a hold. The crowd pushed in, the paddles thwacked. The two painted bodies came to grips, heads on each other's shoulders, hands reaching for a knee, feet trying to trip. They drove against the crowd, bowling onlookers over before the circle re-formed around them. Sweat mixed with the paint on their chests and backs.

Finally one of the warriors managed to grab hold of his opponent's leg and send him tumbling. The crowd swarmed into the circle and lifted the victor high in the air. Looking even more haughty, he was carried in triumph through the admiring throng, followed by the dancing, gleaming girls who sang his name and pierced the air with ululations.

The wrestling went on until dark. Then everyone retreated to Eluheimir, where the drumming, dancing, singing, and drinking continued until the revelers eventually wandered home.

Zaki, an Arab merchant, invited me to drink tea with him on the porch of his shop. I told him and Farouk how glad I was to have been there that day.

"Oh, today was nothing," Farouk told me. "You just wait until tomorrow. People will come from Teis, from Buram, from all over for the big wrestling."

I parked the car in front of Zaki's shop and climbed into the roof tent. But I could not sleep. The sound of drums, songs, and ululations echoed down the hills silhouetted against the starry sky outside the mosquito netting. Just before daybreak, a string of wrestlers danced through the settlement, yelling, "I need chickens, I need milk, I need meat."

At sunrise I was again sipping tea on the porch with Farouk and Zaki. The drumming had stopped; it was quiet for the first time since the previous afternoon. Farouk told me that everyone had gone to sleep.

Later that morning, Nuba women came down from the hills to trade in the shops. One woman brought a gourd of *dura*, for which she received pieces of dried fish, four onions, and a tomato paste can filled with cooking oil that Zaki dipped from a vat. Zaki added the *dura* to the growing mound on his porch.

Dinka man thatching roof, near Malakal.

About 3,000 people gathered for the wrestling matches that afternoon. A dozen or more contests went on simultaneously. Circles formed around two combatants, dissolved, and re-formed for another bout. I was in a sea of whirlpools, pulled from one match to the next, driven back by the leather paddles, and sucked forward into the wake of victory parades.

Night fell, and again everyone moved to the area in front of the shops. There they celebrated until the dancers and drummers tired, and people once more dispersed. After some fish stew with Farouk and Zaki, I went to bed exhausted.

Sometime in the middle of the night, I was awakened by thunderously loud drums. The earth under the car shook. Dazed, I peered out through the mosquito net. A three-quarter moon in the clear sky shone on 300 Nubas dancing in a circle around the car. The white-painted wrestlers and oiled girls shimmered as the drums drove them around and around the car, feet stomping, bells jangling, voices soaring.

Farouk was standing just below my tent. "Come," he said. "Come, they want you to dance."

THE NILE FLOWS 1,100 miles between Juba, the main town in the south, and Khartoum, but drops only 270 feet—about one foot every four miles. In the middle of these clay plains, the drop becomes almost nothing; the Nile spreads out in the Sudd, a Maine-sized morass of constantly shifting papyrus and reeds where one-half its water is lost to evaporation and seepage.

The Sudd, Arabic for barrier, is largely responsible for southern Sudan's isolation. A way through it was not discovered until 1840; a permanent channel was opened only in 1899. Even today, a stern-wheeler trip from north to south can take anywhere from six days to six weeks, depending on how often the boat breaks down, runs aground, or is impeded by vegetation.

The boat I traveled on, the *Hurriya*, was a floating village; three barges were lashed together in front of the stern-wheeler, and one on each side. People, goats, chickens, and sacks of goods crowded the barges' two levels of open deck. Villagers flocked to the boat when we stopped, offering to sell local produce. Passengers cooked their meals and conducted business transactions while we sailed. *Hurriya* was a cumbersome vessel. The only way it maneuvered some of the river bends was by crashing into the bank and reversing several times.

Even when I stood atop the wheel house, 25 feet above the water, the Sudd felt oppressively monotonous. The dark brown Nile disappeared around bends fore and aft, enclosed by 15-foot papyrus and reeds that stretched in a feathery plain from horizon to horizon.

I also saw the Sudd from helicopters, courtesy of Chevron, which at the time was exploring for oil in the swamps. From the air all was water: standing in open lakes, meandering through channels, reflecting the sun from beneath dark green vegetation. Thousands of insect- and fish-eating birds flew up as we passed overhead. Buffalos and Nile lechwes splashed through the swamp. Monitor lizards as big as crocodiles basked on gray anthills jutting from the water.

Certain eroded anthills provided Nuer fishermen just enough room to make camps—two or three mosquito nets, a fire, and a rack to dry strips of fish. Along the swamp's edge, larger islands supported duom palms and the Nuer's chocolate-drop shaped huts. Descending from the reed-fenced compounds were alternately flooded and dry *dura* fields. The scene in northern Sudan was reversed; here was a vast desert of water and green in which the oases were dry and brown.

Nuer man carrying half a Nile perch, Adok.

THE NUER ARE a seminomadic Nilotic tribe who inhabit the Sudd. In the rainy season, they live above the flood plain in family compounds comprised of a large hut, *luok*, where the cattle are kept and the men sleep, and smaller ones, *duel*, which house the women and children. Isolated from other cultures and cut off from each other during the six-month rains, the Nuer have developed a fiercely egalitarian society. There are no chiefs, though ritual leaders and men who have gained status through cattle raiding or other laudable activities may be heeded more than others. But their words bind no one. Decisions affecting groups are made by consensus.

The rains, when pasture and food are limited, are times to be endured. The dry season is the time of plenty. Old people and mothers with small children stay in the compounds with a few milk cows, but everyone else heads off to the *toich*, the seasonal flood plain. Herds of cattle are combined and driven across the *toich*, following the receding water toward permanent swamp. The Nuer congregate in cattle camps.

I was with Peter Kuanen, an old Nuer man I met in the town of Bentiu on the Bahr el Ghazal, a Nile tributary that runs along the Sudd's northern edge. Peter spoke English—he had been to mission school—and offered to "give me some words" about his people. We had driven south from Bentiu and stopped to spend the night at a Nuer compound.

Dinka boy hammering stake to tether ox, cattle camp south of Yirol.

"The wey (cattle camp) is the place just only young people can go, and no eat anymore food [sorghum]," Peter explained. "Nowadays at the wey they don't like food, but are just only drinking milk and eating meat. And also they have to go and fish and come and cook the fish on the fire. They are not cooking it with the pot, no. The pot cannot come to the wey. Just only drink milk and eat meat and fish from the fire. Oh, this way you can be very, very, very fat.

"When they first get to the place where they want to make the wey," Peter went on, "they must kill a cow and pray, so there will be a lot of grass to eat and water to drink, and so the wild animals will not come and eat the cows. They bring those kodar (poles), who are the god of the grass. They have to take them from the luok, where they live when it is raining, and put them in the camp so everything can be all right.

"The old people stay in the houses. And when children are small they stay with their mothers there. When five or six they have to go to the wey. They can milk the cows, and look what the big boys and girls are doing. Oh, the wey is the best place—all the boys and girls can be together and can be dancing in the night. It is making people too much happy."

The Nuer, like the neighboring Dinka and other Nilotic peoples in Sudan, decorate their bodies with patterns of scars. Some are purely ornamental, others the mark of the tribe. When a Nuer boy is initiated into manhood at about age

14, six parallel lines are cut across his forehead from ear to ear.

When a bit older, boys and girls add small, round, ornamental scars to their faces and bodies. These have no ritual significance but, according to Peter, "We make those scars so to be beautiful. Yes, on the face, and the chest also, so that if you are talking with a girl, you can go and touch her on that place so that

you can be very glad, you young man. Even the girl also has to come and touch your chest, and you can be glad for that."

When a Nuer boy has his head cut, he is through with childish things and may no longer milk the cows or sleep in his mother's hut; he spends his nights in the *luok* with the men and cattle. His main interests are looking after the herd, dancing, and sex. He is given a spear and becomes a warrior. His father presents him with an ox, and the new man takes the ox's name. The number of expressions used to describe cattle reflects their importance to the Nuer; hundreds of names refer to bovine colors, patterns, shapes, horns, age, sex, and ear markings. Peter's ox-name is Choriak, "a very big white-and-black bull that has no any horns."

"We will die without the cows," Peter said when I asked him how he felt about the troubles between north and south. "We only need water, grass, a house, and a stable. We do not need anything from the government. We wish they could leave us alone. You see us now; we are walking naked. We do not know anything different. We only want to look after the cows and grow dura.

Murle man celebrating white-eared kob migration, Pibor.

"The people of the north will never treat us well. Even now they still do call us slaves. If a southern man is a government minister even, they do treat him bad. It has always been like this, and I cannot think that it will change ever.

"When I was a small boy, my father told me about an Arab man called Suliman who was carrying people away with a very big canoe which has got big clothes [sails], so that when the wind does come the canoe can move on the water. Those Arabs catch the people and make them walk to that canoe. Then they have to put 50 people inside and 50 on top, and tie them with a rope. Nuer, Dinka, Zande, Shilluk—any kind of people they do take. These people who are tied, if they die, they can just throw them in the river. The ones who reach Khartoum they do sell to other Arabs.

"Now those Arabs want to take the kerosene [oil] away to their country. When we do say, 'No,' then they send the army and kill many people and burn villages near here. Now when you go to sleep at night, the army does go around and listen, and they can take you away or just shoot you. And they take our cows, but we will die without the cows. And they are having our women. How can we have peace when they are doing these things and do not let us alone? Our world has come to nothing."

Early the next morning, Peter, a half-dozen Nuer, and I set off along a narrow, gray footpath that snaked through the golden grasslands. Herds of wildlife and cattle had preceded us, reducing the eight-foot grass to stubby clumps. Thin cracks divided the earth into a jigsaw puzzle of baked clay. A hot wind filled the air with dust and smoke.

We were loaded down with the supplies I needed (or thought I did): camera gear, cans of food, clean drinking water, insect repellent (there are 63 *species* of mosquitos in the Sudd), malaria pills, and other medicines. As we walked, a constant stream of conversation moved up and down the line. It was only music to me, but I could tell one woman was alternately amused and irritated by the slippery aluminum case she carried on her head.

The monotony of the grasslands, the sing-song of the Nuers' voices, the scraping of bare feet on hard clay, and the stupefying heat in-duced in me a sort of trance. Soaked with sweat, my body became an attractive surface for dust and insects.

We crossed two gray, sluggish rivers about waist-deep and 50 yards wide. I realized, as I took off my shoes and stepped

Dinkas in a palm log boat, south of Yirol.

into the slimy bottom, that the reeds and still water signaled the threat of bilharziasis. I had heard that the treatment for this parasitic infection was to give the patient arsenic until he was near death. The parasite, sensing that its host had expired, then died, and the patient was brought back to life.

The Nuer just walked into the river, pausing only to scoop up water to drink. They know about bilharziasis, though understand it in a different way. Like malaria, tuberculosis, dysentery, and high infant mortality, it is as much a part of their environment as pasture and rain. They wanted to get to the cattle camp on the other side of the river, so they waded across, and I followed.

We arrived in the heat of early afternoon. Little distinguished the site from the surrounding plain except that the earth was rubbed bare where hundreds of cattle had trampled the clay into a fine dust. Short stakes where the cattle were tethered at night dotted the ground. Large, smoldering mounds of dung gave off an acrid smoke that, along with the powdery dust, made the air heavy. Clusters of four-foot grass-and-dung huts served as elaborate windscreens. Out-side the huts stood the *kodar* representing the god of grass.

My arrival caused quite a stir. Many of the children had never been so close to a *khawajah* (foreigner) before—some must have never even seen one. I don't know what they were saying about me, but most of the children burst into tears. I must have looked odd; though my 6'5'' height was not unusual to the Nuer, I wore glasses and a shirt which by this time had become rather aromatic, and brown hair grew not only from my head but from my pale body.

"Maleh," I said, trying the little Nuer I had learned. They stared at me in disbelief. What kind of *khawajah* was this who could speak Nuer? When they recovered from the shock, they responded almost in unison with the next phrase.

"Mal-me-dit."

"Mal-me-guah," I replied.

"Mal-me-chum-chum."

Nuer man making a tether, cattle camp near Adok.

It was my turn, but I had exhausted my Nuer vocabulary. They thought it was hilarious. Having tried to learn their language seemed to make up for the fact that I rudely cut short what should be a more elaborate interchange.

One bold young woman reached out and touched the hair on my forearm, then screeched loudly and jerked away as if she had touched a burning ember. She reached out again and rubbed her hand on my arm. She gathered the hair in a bunch, pulling to see how firmly it was attached The rest of the crowd was emboldened, and soon it was mayhem—hands felt my arms, ran through the hair on my head—and the children pulled the hair on my legs.

Most Nuer have no body hair. The ones I met had probably never been free to examine anyone of my hue, or on whom hair grew so profusely, and they were not shy about doing so. In their world, hair covered the bodies of animals.

After a while, they tired of me and dispersed. The cattle and most of the young men were out on the *toich*, and there was not much activity during the heat. The women played with their children or sat and talked. A few of them did chores, scraping hides or cleaning out *diars*, the milking gourds that look like pumpkins with necks.

"These people, they will stay in this camp because there is such much grass here now," said Peter. "But when the grass will be done, then they will have to go far, to the river. They can make a new wey in that place and live there until it is raining again. At that time they have to be going back to their houses. But you can see that everyone is so much happy now to be together."

In the evening, as it got cooler, activity increased. Girls collected dried cow dung and added it to the smoldering fires, filling the air with thick smoke that kept away mosquitos. Toward dusk the cattle were driven in from pasture and walked straight to their tethers, waiting patiently to be tied for the night. The girls and women milked them; the young men gathered to talk. Milk was passed around in small gourds.

"Now they have finished drinking the milk, all of them, and they have to go and dance," Peter told me. "Just only the girls and boys. The girls have gone now to get the beads for their bodies."

A few young men started singing and dancing, jangling the bells around their ankles. More joined in, forming rows of four or five dancers that moved back and forth in unison. The girls appeared, naked except for beaded headbands and belts that bounced softly on their hips. Standing at the periphery at first, the girls eyed the boys, then took up the song and faced them. The opposing lines danced toward each other with short pounding steps and dramatic pelvic thrusts, then backed away. Back and forth they danced, singing alternate verses, the boys challenging the girls, the girls daring the boys.

At about midnight, Peter told me we should move away: "Now is the time these boys and girls they have to go and play. It is no any good for the old people to stay here with them, but to go and sleep."

We retired to the other side of the camp, and lay down next to a smoldering fire. "Now you have seen this wey," Peter said as I drifted off to sleep. "Life should be always like this."

Peter and I walked back to the car the next morning just as the men herded the cattle to pasture. Peter said he wanted to show me something at a place called Duar.

We drove south until we came to a lone fig tree. Pouches of tobacco hung from its limbs, and metal bracelets looped around them. Some had been put on the tree years ago and were half absorbed into it.

"This is the place where our first ancestor, Dja-gay, came up out of the earth," Peter explained. "It is a very, very, very good place, and all the Nuer have to come here and put bracelets and tobacco on the tree for their ancestors, because you know those old people, they do like to smoke. No anybody can come and take the tobacco away, no. They can die if they do."

Nuer woman leading cattle to tether, cattle camp south of Bentiu.

Peter pointed to a pair of small indentations in the earth beneath the tree. "Here," he said. "Can you see these holes? This is made by the knees of the first woman when she gave birth to the first child.

"In March, all the Nuer have to gather here. Too much marissa is made and many cows killed when people come to talk about God, called Maneh. If they do this, everyone will be healthy. No sickness then. Oh, and we do dance very much at this time, and when we are finished dancing, we can come and sleep here under the tree where we were born, and no anything bad can happen to us.

"I have to bring you to this place so that Maneh can help you when you are going to your home that is far."

I LEFT PETER and the Nuer and drove along the construction route of the Jonglei Canal, a deep gash in the plains east of the Sudd. A five-story bucket wheel had dug two-thirds of the 225-mile canal. Attended by a swarm of workers, it loomed over the primeval landscape like a monster, churning and belching exhaust. "It is very strange," said a Nuer man who stopped to stare at the machine. "It picks up the ground from there and puts it in another place. A man

Murle hunters butchering white-eared kob, Pibor.

said they will make a river here, but I think he is trying to fool me. Where will they get the water? The Nile is our river."

Farther south, the Sudd ended and the Nile became a river again. The clay plains met the ironstone plateau. The woodlands became thicker; the firm red earth was flushed with green.

I stopped for a few days in Juba. The town's swelling population stretched its minimal services way beyond capacity. Around the new but already crumbling government buildings and air-conditioned compounds of foreign aid workers spread shantytowns of grass huts with no water or sanitation facilities. The crowded, unhealthy conditions breed epidemics and deep feelings of discontent.

Trade in Juba, and in all of the south, was monopolized by northern merchants who, though not rich, were far better off than the local people. Due to staggering transportation problems, goods were sold for five times their cost in the north, reinforcing southern feelings of exploitation.

"What can we do?" one young southern man asked me. "Do you see steamers bringing goods up the Nile? Do you see hospitals, or schools, or roads, or buses, or factories being built? No. Those Arabs have not changed their attitudes about us, and they never will. Look what Nimeiri is doing now. He has divided the south, gone against the agreement he made with us, and now he wants to make all this a Moslem land. Those Arabs will never help us because we are black and Christian. It is hopeless. What else can we do but fight?"

While I was in Juba, southern units in the army mutinied. Many soldiers and civilians took to the bush, formed a group called the Sudan People's Liberation Army (SPLA), and launched a guerilla war against the government. Angry mobs attacked northern merchants. Foreign relief workers were harassed. Boats stopped traveling the Nile. Later, the rebels attacked Chevron's facilities in the Sudd and the Jonglei Canal machine; both operations have shut down. Nimeiri was overthrown in 1985, but southern Sudan remains enveloped in war, cut off from the rest of the world. It has slipped once again into isolation.

Mondari woman with forehead tribal identification scars and decorative belly button scar, south of Tali Post.

Commencement of the Nuba harvest celebration and wrestling matches, Eluheimir.

Nuba wrestling match, Eluheimir.

Nuba wrestling match, Eluheimir.

116

Shilluk boy leaving his king's cattle hut, Fashoda.

Nile steamer traveling through the Sudd, near Adok.

Nuer fisherman poling a dugout through the Sudd, southwest of Adok.

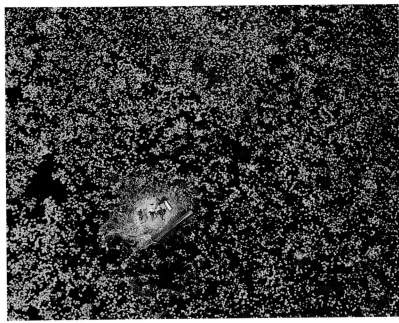

(Top and above) Nuer fishermen camped on eroded anthill, the Sudd.

Nuer homestead, near Adok.

Nuer man weaving duom palm fronds, south of Bentiu.

Dinka cattle camp, near Bor.

124

Dinka cattle camp, near Yirol.

125

Lafon woman grinding sorghum on granite, Lafon.

126

Forestry camp below 8,000-foot Mount Garia, Imatong Mountains.

127

Murle men dancing during the white-eared kob migration, Pibor.

Zande man wearing British campaign medals from World War II, near Yambio.
129

Dinka cattle camp, south of Yirol.

UGANDA AND THE HEADWATERS

The first ten miles of the drive into Uganda did not bode well: deep holes and jagged ruts made it impossible to do more than crawl. I departed Sudan at Nimule, where the Nile carves a wide oxbow before crashing over the Fula rapids. At the border, the track left the river. Dense forest crowded in on me; the air was heavy with impending rain.

My last visit to Uganda had been unpleasant. In 1979, as Tanzanian troops drove Idi Amin out of the country, Dave Wood of *Time*, David Lamb of the *Los Angeles Times*, and I were arrested by Amin's notorious State Research Bureau. We were herded at gunpoint into a low, tin-roofed shack and made to sit in a room smeared with dried blood. The moans of someone being beaten drifted down the dingy hall. A tall, thin man in a blue polyester leisure suit and mirror sunglasses came in, interrogated us for half an hour, then had his lackeys muscle us to individual cells. We each were made to write detailed accounts of who we were, where we came from, and what we were doing there.

"We know you are CIA mercenaries," the man said as he leaned over me, the bare light bulb reflecting in his glasses like tiny yellow eyes. "You must write everything, all of it the truth. If it is not, well, we have ways of making you tell us."

He left me with a pad of paper and a pen. With trembling hand I wrote everything of relevance I could think of. Images of torture and death raced through my mind; the State Research Bureau was nothing more than a gang of executioners. A few weeks earlier, four western journalists had been murdered in Uganda.

Half an hour later the man came back, grabbed the paper, and mouthed what words he could read. Before finishing the first few lines, he threw the paper back at me.

"This is not enough. You must write more."

It seemed he wanted length, so I wrote about the weather, what a beautiful country Uganda is, anything to fill up space.

"This is good now," the man said when he returned. "You come."

I was taken to wait with my friends. We were afraid to look at each other lest we laugh at the C-movie situation or cry because we were so helpless. We could hear our interrogator trying to get through to someone on the phone. It took an awfully long time. Then we heard him yell into the phone, slam the receiver down, and stride toward the room where we were confined. He burst

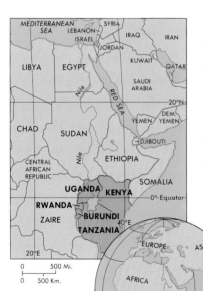

(Facing) Crowned crane.

in with a huge, obsequious grin.

"Oh, my friends. You are free to go now. I hope you know you are always welcome in Uganda."

Amin had since been deposed and the State Research Bureau disbanded, but I was nervous as I entered the country nonetheless. Greater anarchy and brutality had followed Amin's murderous regime. People even spoke of the "good old days when Idi was here."

Uganda is abundantly fertile and beautiful, and its people are friendly and hospitable. But it has been plagued by corrupt leadership and torn apart by tribalism. Once the intellectual and economic center of eastern Africa, Uganda was rich in sophisticated people and agricultural produce. It has also been the scene of some of history's worst atrocities. Uganda is both the Pearl of Africa and the Heart of Darkness.

I drove slowly through the noman's land until a tree trunk barred my way. It was a roadblock; the drunken soldiers manning it lolled in the shade of a tree. They roused themselves when I pulled up and shuffled to the car. Their muddy bootlaces dragged in the dirt, as did the butts of their semiautomatic rifles.

"Get out," one of them yelled. "Let me see your papers."

I did as he ordered. He stared intently at my passport, holding it upside down.

Wallowing hippopotamuses, Queen Elizabeth National Park, Uganda.

"Everything out of the car," he yelled.

The other soldiers had already begun pulling things from the car: cases, jerry cans, tools, spare parts, food. Luckily I had locked some of the cases, but others were soon opened and their contents dumped in the dirt. I could stop the soldiers I actually caught stealing, but while I was engaged with one drunken thief, the others were busy stuffing their pockets.

Finally they were done. I gathered up my belongings and shoved them in the car, not taking time to repack neatly. I just wanted to get out of there.

"Give us medicine," the soldier demanded.

"What kind of medicine?"

"We are suffering very much from malaria, dysentery, and most of all, this gonorrhea."

Gee, that's too bad, I thought, but I said I did not have any medicine for that and got in the car.

"Give us cigarettes."

I drove away, praying they would not shoot at me, or if they did, that they were too drunk to aim. The sigh of relief I heaved as they disappeared from my rearview mirror was premature. A mile down the road was another army roadblock. The same scenario started, except that these soldiers seemed nastier, angry because they were not getting first pick of the loot. One pushed me around with his rifle butt and kicked at my things, which were once again lying in the dirt. He demanded to know why I had so many cameras.

Fortunately, and why I will never know but for which I will always be thankful, the soldier looking over my documents suddenly yelled at the others to leave me alone. He even apologized, trying to make a joke of the whole thing. I laughed with him, jumped in the car, and drove away before he could change his mind.

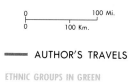

The army, I was to learn later, was the country's biggest problem. With no fear of punishment, the soldiers did whatever they pleased. President Milton Obote dared not discipline the troops; he needed their support.

Several miles later another barrier blocked the road, this time for customs and immigration. The officials were pleasant; the customs man even apologized for making me unpack. My papers were stamped, and I drove the hundred yards to the police barrier. In the hut where I registered myself and the car, I was told the police would have to check my things. I smiled at them. One walked out with me, looked at all the stuff in the car, and asked me what time it was. I told him.

"It is all right," he said. "You just go."

It was lunch time.

I drove south on a road free of barriers to the town of Gulu. Despite political insecurity and a wrecked infrastructure, goods lined the shops, and buses, taxis, and trucks crowded the market. Gulu even had a hotel. But I wanted to get back to the Nile and away from the army, so I left town heading west.

At the roadblock on the edge of Gulu, I picked up a policeman who wanted a ride to his village. "Look at these roads," he said. "They used to be good. Everything went down during Amin's time. He was a very, very bad man. Not a road or school or hospital was built by him. He spent all our money on himself and his army, buying whiskey for them. Look at this land. We could grow anything here. We could be rich, but we cannot find peace."

I dropped the policeman at his home, declining an invitation to tea. I wanted to press on to Murchison Falls National Park before dark. What I had seen and heard of the army made me not want to drive or camp along the road at night.

As I drove into the park, a thunderstorm that had been gathering all afternoon burst. The disused track became a river. Herds of hartebeests and Uganda kob stood motionless on the plains, backs to the howling wind. When I could no longer see the hood of my car, I stopped.

Tanzanian fisherman removes Tilapia *from net, Kagera River.*

That night, as I lay in my tent, I tuned into the BBC. The news from Uganda was of a massacre of 200 people in the Luwero Triangle and men in army uniforms seen dumping 50 bodies into a mass grave.

Straddling the Nile at Lake Albert's northeast end, the park was a haven from violence, but with few inhabitants. Tourists once flocked to see Uganda's abundant wildlife, but the parks provided no shelter for the animals during the years of chaos. Retreating and advancing armies shot for trophies, meat, and target practice. Local people, taking advantage of the situation, poached for food. All the populations were decimated, particularly those of trophy animals. Rhinoceroses, both black and northern white, once abounded. Now there are none.

I was the only guest at Pakuba Lodge. Built during Amin's years as a resort for bigwigs, it has a grand southerly view over Lake Albert's shimmering water and mountains rising to the west, in Zaire. As Amin's army fled from the invading Tanzanians, soldiers looted the lodge.

A small staff was trying to get the lodge going again. Some rooms had been fixed up, and the bar was stocked with French wine, German beer, and Scotch whiskey. A waiter came into my room to light the lamp, a rag stuffed into a small can of kerosene. He wanted to know if I would eat there, since there was no electricity to light the dining room. I said that would be fine.

"But we do not have any food," he said. "I think you will be happy with an omelet."

At Paraa, the park headquarters, I saw Iain Douglas-Hamilton, a Scottish-born wildlife expert I have known for several years. Iain had been monitoring Uganda's elephant population. "In 1973, there were 14,300 elephants in Murchison," he told me. "By 1980, only 1,400 were left. I don't know how many there are now. Gun-toting man has become the dominant ecological factor in this park."

One afternoon we went up in Iain's single-engine plane to look for elephants and poachers. We flew over the southern section of the park, fruitlessly zigzagging above the grassland for about an hour, then crossed the Nile and searched the north. Just as we were ready to give up, Iain spotted about 300 elephants on a marshy plain where the Nile flows out of Lake Albert. That single herd probably contained most of the park's surviving elephants.

From high in the air, the Nile began to make sense to me. In Uganda it is not a single river, but a system that gathers water from central Africa and sends it north. Below us was the Victoria Nile. It flows north from Lake Victoria to Lake Kyoga, bends west, crashes over Murchison Falls, and flows into the northern end of Lake Albert. Lake Albert's southern end is fed by the Semliki River, which drains Lakes Edward and George, both filled by runoff from the Ruwenzori Mountains. From Lake Albert, the Nile emerges as the river I had followed from the Mediterranean Sea.

I spent a few days camping at the top of Murchison Falls, once a popular tourist site. Seven-foot grass grew in the track, railings and signs had fallen over, and the steps leading down the falls had eroded to conform, once more, to the rock from which they were hewn.

An ever-changing rainbow arced in the spray cast up as the river crashed into a gap only 30 feet wide and thundered into the cauldron 130 feet below. The constant roar, the kaleidoscopic patterns of water tumbling against rock were mesmerizing. Only in that spot is the Nile's power so concentrated.

In the afternoons, I clambered down the cliffs and wandered along the riverbank. Black-and-white colobus monkeys feeding in the trees called warnings of my approach. Fat crocodiles some 20 feet long, slipped into the water and turned to watch only nostrils and beady eyes visible above the surface. I heard the deep guffaws of hippos from pools where they waited out the midday heat.

Near my campsite I found a small pool sheltered from the main current by a low shelf of rock. I lay there, letting the water rush over me, unconcerned about hippos and crocs—the current was too swift for them to lurk nearby. But the bank was lined with thick bush, good cover for lions. When I stooped to wash my face and hair, I felt vulnerable, not unlike the antelopes that approach the river nervously, ready to flee at the first suspicious sight, smell, or sound.

Luo man checking fish traps on small stream, near Lake Victoria, Kenya.

TO REACH KAMPALA, I swung to the west; civil war shut off the area north of the city. Near Fort Portal, at the base of the Ruwenzoris, I passed estates once known for their quality tea. Instead of neat rows of low tea bushes, however, I saw forests. The estates had been nationalized by Amin, and the tea had gone wild, growing into useless 20-foot trees.

Kampala looked prosperous from a distance. Houses and shops surrounded a city center defined by a cluster of tall buildings, atop one of which perched a construction crane that lent an air of industry to the town.

Closer inspection revealed a less encouraging picture. Marabou storks, looking like undertakers, stood on the crane; the building seemingly under construction had been abandoned years before. Storks picked at refuse in overflowing dumpsters, moving only slightly when people added to the mounds. Kampala's streets were scarred by grenades, mortars, and rockets. Buildings were pockmarked with bullets, windows shattered or gone. Electricity and phones worked intermittently. Vultures circled overhead and roosted atop the main hospital. Armed troops patrolled the streets by day. Armed gangs, some of them off-duty soldiers, prowled the night.

"The common good has not been so good," one Ugandan businessman told me. "For 20 years, the governments have never done anything for me, not even let me live in peace. How can you feel secure when it is the security forces that are killing you?"

Uganda's is the worst case of the problems besetting modern African nations; it has seen tribalism at its most virulent, corruption at its most venal. Like other African states, Uganda is a country because at the end of the last century, European powers drew some lines on a map. Tribes were separated from traditional allies, thrown together with old enemies, even divided by the new borders. The Africans had no say. Their spears, bows, and arrows were no match for the colonizers' weapons.

Luo boy carrying calf, near Lake Victoria, Kenya.

When the British first visited the area north and west of Lake Victoria, they found something they had seen nowhere else in eastern Africa—large, sophisticated political units, the Bantu kingdoms of Baganda, Bunyoro, Nkole, and Toro. The kings were despotic and often cruel, and the kingdoms were continually at war with one another, but a rough equilibrium between them allowed the people to enjoy a prosperous life founded on the abundance of their fertile and well-watered land.

The Bantu-speaking peoples, who make up about one-half of the area's ethnic groups, have a 2,000-year history in what is now Uganda. The partitioning of Africa threw them together with Nilotic peoples who migrated into the area north of the Nile during the last 500 years. Traditionally, Bantus and Nilotics had little to do with each other. They were separated not only by the Nile and Lake Kyoga, but also by language and culture. In 1894, 40 distinct, independent, and proud groups of people were expected to redefine themselves as citizens of the British Uganda Protectorate.

Pax Britannica was imposed on the kingdoms. Development came quickly to the fertile south. Kampala's Makerere University was a mecca for scholars from all over the continent. The city swelled on a tide of economic activity based on Uganda's agricultural riches; coffee, tea, cotton, and sugar exports earned foreign exchange that financed roads, schools, hospitals, and manufactured goods. Southerners made good livings as farmers, businessmen, bureaucrats, and professionals.

In the north, where the land is poorer, develop-ment was slow. In part to make up for this, and taking advantage of the Nilotic warrior tradition, the British recruited northerners into the army and police. Thus both southerners and northerners had avenues for advancement. As independence approached in 1962, Uganda seemed well on its way to successful nationhood.

But the dream of independence became a nightmare. British-imposed order dissolved as Uganda reverted to ancient rivalries and new ones between Bantus and Nilotics. In control of the armed forces, the northerners were in the best position to seize power.

Adult lions devouring a kill while cubs wait their turn, Ngorongoro Crater, Tanzania.

Milton Obote, a northern Lango, was elected prime minister. He ousted Pres-ident Sir Edward Mutesa, the Baganda's hereditary king, made himself president, and declared a state of emergency in the Baganda area, alienating Uganda's largest and most influential tribe.

Obote's first regime was marked by arrogance and corruption. People inside and out of Uganda rejoiced when his army commander, Idi Amin, overthrew him in 1971. Amin promoted members of his own northern Kakwa tribe within the army and embarked upon his well-publicized reign of terror during which an estimated 300,000 Ugandans were shot, battered, and tortured to death.

Amin also sent Uganda into an economic tailspin. In 1972, he expelled 80,000 Asians, many of whom were third-generation Ugandans. The backbone of the economy, Asians were also easy scapegoats. Amin confiscated their homes, fac-tories, and shops, handing them over to his cronies, often illiterates who simply sold whatever stock was on hand and then abandoned them. The economy ground to a halt.

Tanzanians and the Uganda National Liberation Army (UNLA), made up mostly of northern Langi and Acholi, drove Amin from power in 1979. Obote returned. But the UNLA did not liberate Ugandans from savagery. Things got worse. In 1981, the UNLA sought revenge on Amin's Kakwa and other groups living in Nile Province. Obote's soldiers laid waste the land, slaughtered untold thousands of people, and drove half a million refugees into Sudan and Zaire.

In 1982, the UNLA entered the Luwero Triangle, a wedge of rich farmland in the Buganda area, where rebel groups were fighting to overthrow Obote's regime. Only years later would the world learn of the atrocities committed by the UNLA during that war. They ravaged the countryside and massacred between 200,000 and 500,000 people. The Luwero Triangle was littered with the skulls and bones of its people.

Masai celebrating eunoto, *when warriors become men, Rift Valley, Kenya.*

DURING MOST of the day, Kampala's streets bustled with people. I often sat in small shops, talking with the owners and customers. Conversation always came around to politics and security.

"The rich earth of Uganda is our blessing," one shopkeeper said. "It is forgiving, like we are. But perhaps it is also our curse. If we could not survive, maybe we would not put up with all these horrors."

By late afternoon, few people were on the streets. After dark, no one moved. If someone had a party, his guests slept over. I heard gunfire every night, and in the mornings, stories of robbery, rape, and murder.

Every time I went into the streets to make photographs, I was arrested by plainclothesmen. It became something of a joke; I was always taken to the same official who soon tired of me. The first time was not so funny. I was photographing buildings on the main road when a strong hand gripped my shoulder.

"What are you doing?"

I got out my permit from the Ministry of Information. The man said I should come with him. We went into an office building, climbed four flights of stairs, and entered a small, windowless room. I was told to sit on a wooden bench and wait. A dented pie pan on the dirty floor overflowed with cigarette butts. I was tired of being in rooms with single, bare bulbs.

Another man came into the room.

"Who are you?"

I showed him my papers.

"You are lying," he said. "A paper from them means nothing; they only work for the government. We know what you really are. You better tell us the truth, then it will be easier on you."

I asked him who he thought I was.

"You are a South African mercenary. You are taking those photos of Kampala so you will know the place when you attack." He strutted out of the room, slamming the door. I was in another bad movie.

The two men returned to lead me to a bare office where a man sat at an absolutely empty desk. He looked my permit over, handed it back, told me I had to leave all my exposed and unexposed film with him, and that I could go. My two captors walked me to the street.

"You see," one of them said, "we did not take anything from you, or beat you, or mistreat you. We confiscated your films—yes, that is the right word. But we do not want you to write that you were abused here in Uganda."

One afternoon shortly before I left Kampala, I climbed a hill overlooking the city. A young boy joined me, and we sat talking and watching the buses pour out of town. Suddenly five bursts of automatic-weapon fire ripped the air. I jumped.

"Don't be frightened," the boy said. "That is just Kampala life these days. That was small. Usually it is much bigger, so you think it is thunder."

"But aren't you afraid?" I asked.

"Of course we are afraid. But we do not run anymore. Where could we run to?"

FROM KAMPALA I drove along Lake Victoria's northern shore to Jinja, a thriving industrial town before 1972. Though industry ceased, the town fared better than most. Its location on the lake and proximity to Kenya made Jinja ideal for smuggling, the nation's main economic activity.

After exploring the town for a while, I drove down to a park bordering the Nile where it flows out of Lake Victoria. I had followed the Nile 3,507 miles from its mouth at the Mediterranean Sea through deserts, swamps, and roadblocks. Lake Victoria stretched vast and smooth to the horizon; the Nile poured out between high grassy banks. I walked to a small monument by the water that marked the spot where Speke stood on July 28, 1862, and declared, "The Nile is settled."

By coincidence, I was there on July 28.

LAKE VICTORIA is the Nile's great reservoir. Larger than West Virginia, it gathers water from all directions; the rains that fall on western Kenya's tea estates and Tanzania's

Masai warriors dancing, near Taveta, Kenya.

Serengeti National Park all become water of the Nile. During previous journeys, I traveled extensively in these two other East African countries. Kenya, Tanzania, and Uganda were markedly similar at independence; they shared transportation and telecommunications networks and had a common currency. But they went different ways.

Kenya, the poorest in resources, opted for western-style capitalism which, despite some glaring excesses, has brought stability and prosperity. Services and goods are plentiful throughout most of the country; high-rise Nairobi is a bustling boom town.

Tanzania's President Julius Nyerere chose "African socialism" in which the state plans and controls the economy. But there were too few educated Tanzanians to conceive and run the plan. The economy became a shambles; services were minimal, goods, even staple foods, scarce. Tanzanians speak disdainfully of Kenya as a "dog eat dog world." Kenyans reply that in Tanzania the dogs have nothing to eat.

Uganda just fell apart.

El Molo man spearfishing from duom palm log raft, Lake Turkana, Kenya.

THE SOURCE of the Nile is reckoned to be the river that feeds more water into Lake Victoria than any other, the Kagera, which flows into the lake from Rwanda and Burundi.

I followed the Kagera through these two tiny, thickly settled countries, past the Hutus' farms and the Tutsis' grazing herds of cattle. In southern Burundi, more than 4,000 river miles from the Mediterranean, I came to a hill atop which was a small stone pyramid with a plaque that read, *Caput Nili* (Source of the Nile).

I was determined to drive the car up the crumbling track to the pyramid. It seemed fitting that, having traveled so far, the car and I should arrive at the beginning together. Near the top the earth gave way, lifting the left front tire about two feet into the air. I was afraid to move lest my shifting weight send the car tumbling. I had followed the Nile for thousands of miles with no major mishap and was about to blow it only a few yards from the source.

I yelled for help. A group of children playing nearby came scrambling up and stared at me. They said they wanted money. "Fine," I said. "Just all of you climb onto the front of the car." With the kids as counterweight, the car tilted level, and I gave them a ride to the top.

North of the pyramid, a stream laced through brown hills that disappeared into a hazy horizon. I had been thinking about the spring that fed it—the goal of my journey—for months. While slogging through the northern Sudan desert, I pictured a fountain of pure, cool water bubbling from the earth. I envisioned a glade shaded by luxuriant foliage, where wild animals of every species came to drink. A Nubian in Akasha had told me that the Nile was "the river that comes from Paradise," and so I imagined it.

But the source of the Nile no longer bubbles from the earth. A trickle of water issues from a one-inch lead pipe stuck in the low wall of a dirty cement trough. The spring had been "improved."

THE SPRING IS the southernmost source, the beginning of the Victoria system of the Nile. I wanted to see the Albert system's origin as well, so I retraced my steps north to Uganda's Ruwenzoris, the fabled Mountains of the Moon.

In about 150 A.D., the Greek geographer Ptolemy drew a map of the world. Central Africa was a terra incognita, but he imagined the Nile arising in that unknown land and drew as its source two lakes watered by a range of mountains which he labeled the *Lunae Montes*. Although no records indicate travelers had seen the source of the Nile at that time, something led Ptolemy to record a remarkably accurate image. Victoria and Albert could well be his two lakes, and

Turkana children carrying fish, Lake Turkana, Kenya.

when Henry Morton Stanley "discovered" the Ruwenzoris in 1888, it was only fitting they be called the Mountains of the Moon.

The Ruwenzoris, unlike East Africa's two famous mountains, Kenya and Kilimanjaro, are not isolated peaks, but a range 70 miles long and 30 wide. In the center of the range, six peaks bear permanent snow and glaciers, right on the equator. Glacial melt and 75 inches of annual rainfall rush down the mountains in rivulets and streams that feed Lakes Edward, George, and Albert. The Nile begins here at 16,763 feet — as ice.

I spent ten days climbing the Ruwenzoris, setting off from the roadhead where I hired porters and a guide. We followed the course of the Bujuku River, hiking deep gorges crowded with forests, nettles, bushes, and ferns. I stopped (any excuse to rest) to watch a troop of rare Ruwenzori colobus monkeys jumping from tree to tree. I heard a chimpanzee call, but saw no other sign of wildlife. When I rounded a corner on the narrow path and encountered a group of hunters, the reason became clear. They, like my porters, were Bakonjo people who farm the lower slopes and hunt higher up. Elephants, buffalos, leopards, and other animals once roamed the mountains, but long ago were eliminated from all but the most inaccessible parts of their range. The hunters were returning to their village with several trapped hyrax, a rabbit-sized mammal which looks like a rodent but is the elephant's closest living relative. They said very few were left.

As we ascended, the ground became increasingly wet, the air cold. We made camp the second night at 10,900 feet, at Nyamuleju (the place of the beards), where Spanish-mosslike lichen dripped from trees of giant heather. Giant lobelias and giant groundsels, relatives of the common North American plants, grew to enormous size. The spindly lobelias rose 20 feet and stood like sentinels on the mist-covered slopes.

The boggy ground soaked my feet and lower legs in near-freezing water. I saw the sun only once, briefly. The rest of the time rain and thick fog cut visibility to a few yards and chilled me to the bone. For months I had been in climates that required no more than shorts and T-shirts. Except for gloves and a down jacket, I was ill-prepared. My sneakers were wet for ten days. The thought of putting them on my warm feet made it hard to crawl out of the sleeping bag in the mornings.

Life flourished in that weird environment: waterlogged, on the equator, but high, so that solar radiation is intense and temperature variations between night and day extreme. Mosses of brilliant green, crimson, brown, and gold covered rocks and tree trunks. Bushes of everlasting flowers grew where lobelias and groundsels did not.

Saint-John's-wort and Lower Kitandara Lake, Ruwenzori Mountains, Uganda.

Following what had become a rivulet, the path climbed a gap at one end of a long, oval valley. Rocky walls towered above, their steep faces long ago stripped of the soil which had washed down to create an enormous bog dotted with the tussocks of sedge I used as jumping stones to avoid sinking.

One morning at 13,050 feet, I awoke to find the groundsel-studded valley dusted white with snow. Later in the day the sky cleared for the first time, and I could see the peaks of the Ruwenzoris—Mounts Stanley, Baker, and Speke.

The fog swirled back in, obscuring the path to the base of the glaciers. Neither the porters nor I were equipped to attempt them, so we descended, following another watercourse. Often the path was the streambed itself, steep and wet, but the only route through the vegetation.

The last night we camped beneath an overhang under a waterfall that shot over our heads and fell 50 feet. I lay tucked up against the rock, watching the thinning clouds sweep past a full moon that lit the jagged peaks. The cold night air was filled with the roar of water seeking the level of the sea.

From my shelter high on the equator, I thought about the journey the Nile makes, about the countless lives and ways of life it has nurtured and sustains. The Nile is a thread that connects the African and Arab worlds, the present with the ancient past. Though Europeans discovered the source of the Nile only in 1862, it struck me that perhaps a clue existed long, long before. Almost 5,000 years ago, near the mouth of the Nile, the pharaohs built mountains encased in gleaming stone, the Great Pyramids. They stand today, a mirror image of those gleaming white peaks at the other end of the Nile where I fell asleep, in the Mountains of the Moon.

Giant lobelia, near Freshfield Pass, Ruwenzori Mountains, Uganda.

Elephant herd and egrets, Murchison Falls National Park, Uganda.

Lioness with her cubs, Ngorongoro Crater, Tanzania.

Lion males, Masai Mara Reserve, Kenya.

Wildebeest migration, Masai Mara Reserve, Kenya.

Wildebeest migration crossing the Mara River, Masai Mara Reserve, Kenya.

Cheetah female and cub, Masai Mara Reserve, Kenya.

Hyena, Ngorongoro Crater, Tanzania.

Hyenas on a kill, Ngorongoro Crater, Tanzania.

Baganda woman weaving basket, northeast of Kampala, Uganda.

Baganda children among matoke *(cooking banana) stalks, Kome Island, Lake Victoria, Uganda.*

Tea plucker, Kericho, Kenya.

Workers plucking tea, Kericho, Kenya.

Fishing boats on Lake Victoria, near Kisumu, Kenya.

Cascading stream, Ruwenzori Mountains, Uganda.

161

Great Pyramids, Egypt.

(Pages 162-163) Ruwenzori Mountains, Uganda-Zaire border.